2012 EDITION

101 best campsites by the beach

alan rogers

Compiled by: Alan Rogers Guides Ltd

Designed by: Vine Design Ltd

Published by: Alan Rogers Guides Ltd,
Spelmonden Old Oast, Goudhurst, Kent TN17 1HE

www.alanrogers.com
Tel: 01580 214000

British Library Cataloguing-in-Publication Data:
A catalogue record for this book is available from the British Library.

ISBN 978-1-906215-59-0

Printed in Great Britain by
Stephens & George Print Group

contents

Welcome to the Alan Rogers
'101' **guides**

The Alan Rogers guides have been helping campers and caravanners make informed decisions about their holiday destinations since 1968. Today, whether online or in print, Alan Rogers still provides an independent, impartial view, with detailed reports, on each campsite.

With so much unfiltered, unqualified information freely available, the Alan Rogers perspective is invaluable to make sure you make the right choice for your holiday.

What is the '101' **series**?

At Alan Rogers, we know that readers have many and diverse interests, hobbies and particular requirements. And we know that our guides, featuring a total of some 3,000 campsites, can provide a bewildering choice from which it can be difficult to produce a shortlist of possible holiday destinations.

The Alan Rogers 101 guides are devised as a means of presenting a realistic, digestible number of great campsites, featured because of their suitability to a given theme.

This book remains first and foremost an authoritative guide to excellent campsites which offer great seaside holidays.

101 **Best campsites by the beach**

For many, a holiday is not a holiday unless a beach is involved. And none more so than camping holidays. The archetypal sun, sea and sand holiday is, for some, the ideal; for others it's dramatic blustery seascapes and clattering, pebble beaches; yet others prefer secluded little coves and rocky inlets.

Whichever you prefer, this guide features campsites that offer all kinds of beach. There are even wonderful campsites set beside magnificent lakes, complete with their own beach.

So whether you're planning an out-of-season, invigorating seaside break or the full, sandy, bucket and spade extravaganza this summer, read on. There are 101 campsites in this guide and, depending on what kind of beach you're looking for, you are sure to find your ideal holiday destination here.

Alan Rogers – in search of **'the best'**

Alan Rogers himself started off with the very specific aim of providing people with the necessary information to allow them to make an informed decision about their holiday destination. Today we still do that with a range of guides that now covers Europe's best campsites in 27 countries.

We work with campsites all day, every day. We visit campsites for inspection purposes (or even just for pleasure!). We know campsites 'inside out'.

We know which campsites would suit active families; which are great for get-away-from-it-all couples; we know which campsites are planning super new pool complexes; which campsites offer a fantastic menu in their on-site restaurant; which campsites allow you to launch a small boat from their slipway; which campsites have a decent playing area for kicking a ball around; which campsites have flat, grassy pitches and which have solid hard standings.

We also know which are good for fishing, golf, spas, children, nature and outdoor activities; which are close to the beach; and which welcome dogs. These particular themes form our '101' series.

All Alan Rogers guides (and our website) are respected for their independent, impartial and honest assessment. The reviews are prose-based, without overuse of indecipherable icons and symbols. Our simple aim is to help guide you to a campsite that matches best your requirements – often quite difficult in today's age of information overload.

What is the **best**?

The criteria we use when inspecting and selecting sites are numerous, but the most important by far is the question of good quality. People want different things from their choice of campsite, so campsite 'styles' vary dramatically: from small peaceful campsites in the heart of the countryside, to 'all singing, all dancing' sites in popular seaside resorts.

The size of the site, whether it's part of a chain or privately owned, makes no difference in terms of it being required to meet our exacting standards in respect of its quality and it being 'fit for purpose'. In other words, irrespective of the size of the site, or the number of facilities it offers, we consider and evaluate the welcome, the pitches, the sanitary facilities, the cleanliness, the general maintenance and even the location.

Expert opinions

We rely on our dedicated team of Site Assessors, all of whom are experienced campers, caravanners or motorcaravanners, to visit and recommend campsites. Each year they travel around Europe inspecting new campsites for Alan Rogers and re-inspecting the existing ones.

When planning your **holiday...**

A holiday should always be a relaxing affair, and a campsite-based holiday particularly so. Our aim is for you to find the ideal campsite for your holiday, one that suits your requirements. All Alan Rogers guides provide a wealth of information, including some details supplied by campsite owners themselves, and the following points may help ensure that you plan a successful holiday.

Find out more

An Alan Rogers reference number (**eg FR 12345**) is given for each campsite and can be useful for finding more information and pictures online at **www.alanrogers.com**

Simply enter this number in the 'Campsite Search' field on the Home page.

Campsite descriptions

We aim to convey an idea of its general appearance, 'feel' and features, with details of pitch numbers, electricity, hardstandings etc.

Facilities

We list specific information on the site's facilities and amenities and, where available, the dates when these facilities are open (if not for the whole season). Much of this information is as supplied to us and may be subject to change. Should any particular activity or aspect of the campsite be important to you, it is always worth discussing with the campsite before you travel.

Swimming pools

Opening dates, any charges and levels of supervision are provided where we have been notified. In some countries (notably France) there is a regulation whereby Bermuda-style shorts may not be worn in swimming pools (for health and hygiene reasons). It is worth ensuring that you do take 'proper' swimming trunks with you.

Charges

Those given are the latest provided to us, usually 2011 prices, and should be viewed as a guide only.

Toilet blocks

We assume that toilet blocks will be equipped with a reasonable number of British style WCs, washbasins and hot showers in cubicles. We also assume that there will be an identified chemical toilet disposal point, and that the campsite will provide water and waste water drainage points and bin areas. If not the case, we comment. We do mention certain features that some readers find important: washbasins in cubicles, facilities for babies, facilities for those with disabilities and motorcaravan service points.

Reservations

Necessary for high season (roughly mid-July to mid-August) in popular holiday areas (i.e. beach resorts). You can reserve many sites via our own Alan Rogers Travel Service or through other tour operators. Remember, many sites are closed all winter and you may struggle to get an answer.

Telephone numbers

All numbers assume that you are phoning from within the country in question. From the UK or Ireland, dial 00, then the country's prefix (e.g. France is 33), then the campsite number given, but dropping the first '0'.

Opening dates

Dates given are those provided to us and can alter before the start of the season. If you intend to visit shortly after a published opening date, or shortly before the closing date, it is wise to check that it will actually be open at the time required. Similarly some sites operate a restricted service during the low season, only opening some of their facilities (e.g. swimming pools) during the main season; where we know about this, and have the relevant dates, we indicate it; again, if you are at all doubtful it is wise to check.

Accommodation

Over recent years, more and more campsites have added high quality mobile homes, chalets, lodges, gites and more. Where applicable we indicate what is available and you'll find details online.

Special Offers

Some campsites have taken the opportunity to highlight a special offer. This is arranged by them and for clarification please contact the campsite direct.

Life's **a beach**

The lure of the coast, and the beach in particular, is a strong holiday motivation. Most people enjoy a holiday beside the sea, and the many facets a beach has to offer holidaymakers of all ages. There are thousands of campsites across Europe, with many on or close to a great beach either on the coast or beside a shimmering lake. This guide features a short-list of just 101, so read on and start dreaming…

Why the beach...?

In the UK, it was not until the advent of the train in the late 19th century that the masses began to enjoy the benefits of a seaside holiday, fuelling growth of long piers. Later, from the 1920s, glamour became part of the mix, with the south of France attracting the likes of Hemingway and Picasso. An hotel was encouraged to stay open all summer and the Côte d'Azur has never looked back. Venerable fashionable resorts (Biarritz, La Baule) are still going strong; sandy expanses in the West Country are perennial favourites; the blustery Scandanavian beaches are atmospheric and unspoilt; and the vast sandy beaches of the Spanish Costas offer a special magic.

Finding the right **beach campsite**

Sun, sea and sand...it sounds simple but finding the right balance can be difficult with a campsite beach holiday. Some people want to be right there in the action, right on the beach; others prefer a campsite that's set back from the hurly-burly, even if it means a short drive. Some simply want miles of sand, with or without the crowds, others search for secluded rocky coves, perhaps seeking out that perfect spot beneath a shady pine.

You will find campsites with majestic sweeping sea views, campsites which run regular shuttle buses to and from the beach – especially handy when parking is at a premium; some campsites have their very own private stretch of beach and this may vary between sand, shingle, craggy rocks and dunes.

Quality Beaches

What makes a good beach? Which is the best beach in the area? Which beach is best for children? These are all valid questions but everyone will have their own opinion.

Blue Flag

Blue Flag is a prestigious international award scheme for beaches which acts as a guarantee of quality. Awarded annually to over 3,450 beaches and marinas in 41 countries, the award of a Blue Flag is based on compliance with 32 criteria covering the aspects of:

- Environmental Education and Information
- Water Quality
- Environmental Management
- Safety and Services

Children on **beaches**

Family memories are made of long sunny days at the beach: splashing in the shallows, sandcastles, sandy sandwiches, buckets of crabs.

A good family beach, especially for young children, will have clean sand (ideally of the kind that makes good sandcastles), gently sloping down to the sea. Hopefully the sea at low tide is not a mile away, allowing toddlers to paddle while remaining close by (although a lovely wide beach does allow plenty of room for games and kite flying). And of course an ice cream vendor can usually bring a few squeals of pleasure!

Activities for children

Some larger beaches often have activities specially for children, usually in high season – these could range from playgrounds or boating lakes right up to paid-for clubs with organised activities all day. And of course, in the UK the traditional donkey ride still exists!

For the younger ones

- Dig a channel to the sea
- Make a dam
- Bury dad in the sand
- Go beach combing for the most interesting "find"
- Build a boat or a car in the sand big enough to sit in – always makes an amusing snap for the album!

Ping Pong Ball Race

Dig a series of sloping channels wide enough (and smooth enough) to take a ping pong ball. Place ping pong balls at the start line and then race each other, blowing the ball down the channel to the finish line.

Beach Mini Golf

Create your own mini golf course in the sand. Players take turns with a plastic golf club and ball - or whatever implement you can find.

Frisbee

A perennial favourite. Set up some targets in the sand and see who can get closest, or arrange plastic bottles in the sand and try to knock them over.

Go prepared and keep a bat and ball in the car – there's always a demand for French cricket, boules, badminton and kite flying.

Water Fun

Many lakeside campsites, especially in Austria, Hungary and Slovenia, have pedaloes, row boats and floating pontoons, as well as on-shore activities.

Activities

on the **beach**

With a bracing breeze, a good boost of ozone and loads of space, a beach always seems to invite activity. It could be a fairly sedate activity like beach combing, throwing the odd stick for the dog or flying a kite. Fishing too is popular, available all year, and for free.

More strenuous and physical activities might include power kiting and sand yachting – popular on the long, wide, flat sandy beaches.

Surfing

By definition, good surfing beaches will involve turbulent waters so try and surf where a lifeguard is present and not on your own. Only surf within your own ability and experience, making sure you are surfing in safe locations.

Kayaking

A great way to spend time on the water but don't take this too lightly – you should be familiar with the necessary kit and precautions. Check the weather, wind and tides, wear a buoyancy aid and ideally paddle in a group, telling someone back on land where you are going. Make sure you can get back on board your kayak should you capsize.

Staying safe at the beach

Beaches are a fun environment but it pays to be aware of potential dangers. In particular, keep an eye on tides – incoming tides can quickly trap people in coves or under cliffs. If unsure, check with a lifeguard. The RNLI beach safety tips are applicable anywhere.

Top Tips

- Always swim at a lifeguarded beach
- Swim between the red and yellow flags *(UK)*
- Never swim alone
- Never use inflatables in strong winds or rough seas
- If you get into trouble, wave and call for help
- If you see someone else in trouble, tell a lifeguard or call emergency services
- Take note of warnings and notices

Enjoy...!

Whether you're an 'old hand' or are contemplating your first trip, a regular reader of our Guides or a new 'convert', we wish you well in your travels and hope we have been able to help in some way. We are, of course, also out and about ourselves, visiting sites, talking to owners and readers, and generally checking on standards and new developments. We hope to bump into you!

Wishing you thoroughly enjoyable camping and caravanning in 2012 – favoured by good weather of course!

The Alan Rogers Team

Further **information**

www.goodbeachguide.co.uk

Website of the Marine Conservation Society

www.blueflag.org

The international organisation responsible for awarding the Blue Flag for beaches (and marinas)

www.onbeach.nl

Dutch website with information and lists of European beaches

www.maplage.fr

French website with extensive information on French beaches

www.esplaya.com

English-language website on the many beaches in Spain

www.italyheaven.co.uk

English-language website on the beaches of Italy

www.kustgids.nl and www.holland.com

Respectively, a Dutch and an English-language website on the beaches of the Netherlands

SPAIN – Sant Pere Pescador

Kawan Village L'Amfora

Avenida Josep Tarradellas, 2, E-17470 Sant Pere Pescador (Girona)
t: **972 520 540** e: **info@campingamfora.com**
alanrogers.com/ES80350 www.campingamfora.com

Accommodation: ☑ Pitch ☑ Mobile home/chalet ☐ Hotel/B&B ☐ Apartment

This super, spacious site is family run and friendly. A Greek theme is evident, mainly in the restaurant and around the pool areas. The site is spotlessly clean, well maintained and aims to be environmentally friendly. There are 830 level, grass pitches (741 for touring) laid out in a grid system, all with 10A electricity. Attractive trees and shrubs have been planted around each pitch. There is good shade in the more mature areas and these pitches include 64 large pitches (180 sq.m), each with an individual sanitary unit (toilet, shower and washbasin). The newer area is more open with less shade and you can choose which you would prefer. Three excellent sanitary blocks (one heated) are fully equipped and offer free hot water, each with staff on almost permanent duty to ensure very high standards are maintained. Access is good for disabled visitors. At the entrance a terraced bar and two restaurants overlook a smart pool complex that includes three pools for children, one with two water slides.

Special offers

Low season offers for senior citizens (pitch): 10=9 / 14=12 / 18=14 / 22=15. Low season Accommodation offers: 7=5 14=10.

You might like to know

There is a large beach club bar, a kite- and windsurfing school and catamarans for hire on the beach.

- ☑ **Beach on site**
- ☐ **Beach within 1 km**
- ☑ **Sandy beach**
- ☑ **Blue Flag quality**
- ☑ **Lifeguardåœ**
- ☐ **Sun lounger and/or deckchair hire**
- ☑ **Watersports** *(e.g. sailing or windsurfing)*
- ☑ **Snacks and drinks**
- ☐ **Sunshades/sunbeds**
- ☑ **Dogs allowed** *(on the beach)*

Facilities: Three main toilet blocks have washbasins in cabins and free showers. Baby rooms. Laundry facilities. Motorcaravan services. Supermarket. Terraced bar, self-service and waiter service restaurants. Pizzeria/takeaway. Restaurant and bar on the beach with limited menu (high season). Disco bar. Swimming pools (1/5-30/9). Pétanque. Tennis. Bicycle hire. Minigolf. Play area. Miniclub. Entertainment. Windsurfing. Boat launching and sailing. Fishing. Exchange facilities. Games and TV rooms. WiFi. Car wash. Torches required in beach areas.
Off site: Riding 4 km. Golf 15 km.

Open: 16 April - 30 September.

Directions: Sant Pere Pescador is on the coast between Roses and L'Escala. From the north on A17/E15 take exit 3 onto N11 towards Figueres then onto the C260 towards Roses. At Castello d'Empúries turn right onto GIV-6216 to Sant Pere. Site is well signed in the town towards the beach. GPS: 42.18147, 3.10405

Charges guide

Per unit incl. 2 persons and electricity	€ 25,00 - € 54,70
extra person	€ 4,50 - € 6,20
child (2-9 yrs)	free - € 4,20

No credit cards.

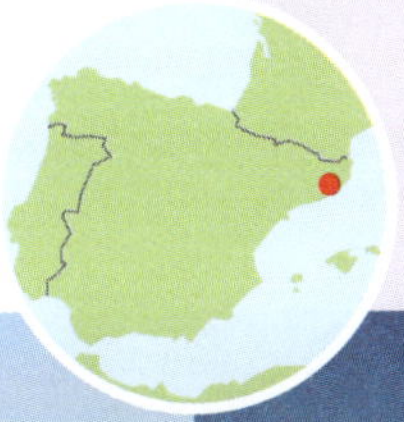

SPAIN – Sant Pere Pescador

Camping Las Dunas

Ctra San Marti - Sant Pere, E-17470 Sant Pere Pescador (Girona)
t: **972 521 717** e: **info@campinglasdunas.com**
alanrogers.com/ES80400 **www.campinglasdunas.com**

Accommodation: ☑ Pitch ☑ Mobile home/chalet ☐ Hotel/B&B ☐ Apartment

Las Dunas is an extremely large, impressive and well organised resort style site with many on-site activities and an ongoing programme of improvements. It has direct access to a superb sandy beach that stretches along the site for nearly a kilometre with a windsurfing school and beach bar. There is also a much used, huge swimming pool, plus a large double pool for children. Las Dunas is very large, with 1,700 individual hedged pitches (1,479 for tourers) of around 100 sq.m. laid out on flat ground in long, regular parallel rows. All have electricity (6/10A) and 180 also have water and drainage. Shade is available in some parts of the site. Much effort has gone into planting palms and new trees here and the results are very attractive. The large restaurant and bar have spacious terraces overlooking the swimming pools, and you can enjoy a pleasant, more secluded, cavern style pub. A disco club is close by in a soundproofed building (people leaving during the night can be a problem for pitches in the central area of the site).

You might like to know

All types of adventure sports are on offer, including canoeing, hot-air balloon excursions, monoplane flights and gliding.

- ☑ **Beach on site**
- ☐ **Beach within 1 km**
- ☑ **Sandy beach**
- ☐ **Blue Flag quality**
- ☑ **Lifeguard** *(high season)*
- ☐ **Sun lounger and/or deckchair hire**
- ☑ **Watersports** *(e.g. sailing or windsurfing)*
- ☑ **Snacks and drinks**
- ☐ **Sunshades/sunbeds**
- ☐ **Dogs allowed** *(on the beach)*

Facilities: Five excellent large toilet blocks (resident cleaners 07.00-21.00). British style toilets (no seats), controllable hot showers and washbasins in cabins. Facilities for youngsters, babies and disabled campers. Laundry facilities. Motorcaravan services. Supermarket, boutique and other shops. Large bar with terrace. Large restaurant. Takeaway. Ice cream parlour. Beach bar in main season. Disco club. Swimming pools. Playgrounds. Tennis. Archery. Sailing/windsurfing Minigolf. school and other watersports. Activity programme, partly in English (15/6-31/8). ATM. Internet café. WiFi. Dogs taken in one section. Torches required. Off site: L'Escala 5 km. Riding and boat launching 5 km. Water park 10 km. Golf 30 km.

Open: 19 May - 2 September.

Directions: L'Escala is northeast of Girona between Palamós and Roses. From the A7/E15 autostrada take exit 5 towards L'Escala on the GI 623. Turn north 2 km. before L'Escala towards Sant Marti d'Ampúrias. Site well signed.
GPS: 42.16098, 3.13478

Charges guide

Per unit incl. 2 persons and electricity	€ 21,00 - € 59,20
extra person	€ 3,50 - € 5,75
child (3-10 yrs)	€ 3,00 - € 3,25

SPAIN – Calonge

Camping Internacional de Calonge

Ctra San Feliu/Guixols - Palamós km 7.6, E-17251 Calonge (Girona)
t: **972 651 233** e: **info@intercalonge.com**
alanrogers.com/ES81300 www.intercalonge.com

Accommodation: ☑ Pitch ☑ Mobile home/chalet ☐ Hotel/B&B ☐ Apartment

This spacious, well laid out site has access to a fine beach via a footbridge over the coast road, or you can take the little road train as the site is on very sloping ground. Calonge is a family site with two good sized pools on different levels, a paddling pool and large sunbathing areas. A great restaurant, bar and snack bar are by the pool. The site's 793 pitches are on terraces, all with electricity (5A), and 84 are fully serviced. The pitches are set on attractively landscaped terraces (access to some may be challenging). There is good shade from the tall pine trees and some views of the sea through the foliage. The upper levels are taken by a tour operator and mobile home pitches. The pools are overlooked by the restaurant terraces with great views over the mountains. A nature area within the site is used for walks and picnics. A separate area is set aside for visitors with dogs (including a dog shower!) The beach is accessed over the main road by 100 steps and is shared with another campsite.

Special offers

For this year's special offers, contact the campsite.

You might like to know

Visit magical cities such as Barcelona, Girona and Figueres, where you can choose from a vast range of cultural, sporting and leisure activities. Or get away from it all with a walk on the beautiful coastal path.

- ☐ **Beach on site**
- ☑ **Beach within 1 km**
- ☑ **Sandy beach**
- ☑ **Blue Flag quality**
- ☑ **Lifeguard** *(high season)*
- ☐ **Sun lounger and/or deckchair hire**
- ☑ **Watersports** *(e.g. sailing or windsurfing)*
- ☑ **Snacks and drinks**
- ☑ **Sunshades/sunbeds**
- ☐ **Dogs allowed** *(on the beach)*

Facilities: Generous sanitary provision in new and renovated blocks include some washbasins in cabins. No toilet seats. One block is heated in winter. Laundry facilities. Motorcaravan services. Gas supplies. Shop (26/3-30/10), Restaurant (1/2-31/12). Bar, patio bar with pizzas and takeaway (27/3-24/10, weekends for the rest of the year). Swimming pools (26/3-16/10). Playground. Electronic games. Rather noisy disco twice weekly (but not late). Bicycle hire. Tennis. Hairdresser. ATM. Internet access and WiFi. Torches necessary in some areas. Road train from the bottom of the site to the top in high season. Off site: Bus at the gate. Fishing 300 m. Supermarket 500 m. Golf 3 km. Riding 10 km.

Open: All year.

Directions: Site is on the inland side of the coast road between Palamós and Platja d'Aro. Take the C31 south to the 661 at Calonge. Follow signs to the C253 towards Platja d'Aro and on to site which is well signed. GPS: 41.83333, 3.08417

Charges guide

Per unit incl. 2 persons and electricity	€ 20,25 - € 47,70
extra person	€ 3,70 - € 8,35
child (3-10 yrs)	€ 1,85 - € 4,55

No credit cards.

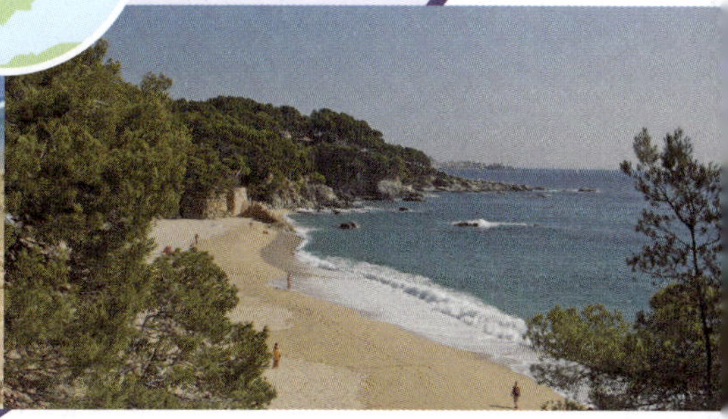

SPAIN – Tossa de Mar

Camping Cala Llevadó

Ctra GI-682 de Tossa a Lloret pk. 18,9, E-17320 Tossa de Mar (Girona)
t: **972 340 314** e: **info@calallevado.com**
alanrogers.com/ES82000 www.calallevado.com

Accommodation: ☑ Pitch ☑ Mobile home/chalet ☐ Hotel/B&B ☐ Apartment

For splendour of position, Cala Llevadó can compare with almost any in this guide. A beautifully situated cliff-side site, enjoying fine views of the sea and coast below. It is shaped something like half a bowl with steep slopes. High up on the site, with a superb aspect, is the attractive restaurant/bar with a large terrace overlooking the pleasant swimming pool directly below. There are terraced, flat areas for caravans and tents (with 10/16A electricity) on the upper levels of the two slopes, with a great many individual pitches for tents scattered around the site. Some of these pitches have fantastic settings and views. In some areas cars may be required to park separately. Many of the 577 touring pitches are available for caravans. There are a few tour operator pitches (45) and 26 bungalows. The steepness of the site would make access difficult for disabled visitors or those with limited mobility. One beach has watersports within a buoyed area and there is a subaqua diving school.

You might like to know

There are some beautiful beaches within easy reach, in one of the most scenic parts of the Costa Brava.

- ☑ **Beach on site**
- ☐ **Beach within 1 km**
- ☑ **Sandy beach**
- ☐ **Blue Flag quality**
- ☐ **Lifeguard** *(high season)*
- ☐ **Sun lounger and/or deckchair hire**
- ☑ **Watersports** *(e.g. sailing or windsurfing)*
- ☑ **Snacks and drinks**
- ☐ **Sunshades/sunbeds**
- ☐ **Dogs allowed** *(on the beach)*

Facilities: Four very well equipped toilet blocks are immaculately maintained and well spaced around the site. Baby baths. Laundry facilities. Motorcaravan services. Gas supplies. Fridge hire. Large supermarket. Restaurant/bar (5/5-28/9). Swimming and paddling pools. Three play areas. Botanic garden. Entertainment for children (4-12 yrs). Sailing, water skiing and windsurfing school. Fishing. Excursions. Internet access and WiFi. Torches definitely needed in some areas. Off site: Bicycle hire 3 km. Riding 10 km. Large complex adjacent for sports activities and swimming.

Open: 1 May - 30 September.

Directions: Cala Llevadó is southeast of Girona on the coast. Leave the AP7/E15 at exit 7 to the C65 Sant Feliu road and then take C35 southeast to the GI 681 to Tossa de Mare. Site is signed off the GI 682 Lloret - Tossa road at km. 18.9, about 3 km. from Tossa. Route avoids difficult coastal road. GPS: 41.71282, 2.90623

Charges guide

Per unit incl. 2 persons and electricity (6A)	€ 29,00 - € 49,30
extra person	€ 5,80 - € 9,75
child (4-12 yrs)	€ 3,35 - € 5,20
dog	€ 4,70 - € 4,90

SPAIN – Salou

Camping Resort Sangulí Salou

Paseo Miramar – Plaza Venus, Apdo 123, E-43840 Salou (Tarragona)
t: **977 381 641** e: **mail@sanguli.es**
alanrogers.com/ES84800 www.sanguli.es

Accommodation: ☑ Pitch ☑ Mobile home/chalet ☐ Hotel/B&B ☐ Apartment

Sangulí is a superb site boasting excellent pools and entertainment for the whole family. Owned, developed and managed by a local Spanish family, it has something for everyone, with everything open when the site is open. There are 1,067 pitches of varying size (75-100 sq.m) and all have electricity. Mobile homes occupy 58 pitches and there are fully equipped bungalows on 147. A wonderful selection of trees, palms and shrubs provides natural shade and an ideal space for children to play. The good sandy beach is little more than 100 metres across the coast road and a small railway crossing. Although large, Sangulí has a pleasant, open feel and maintains a quality family atmosphere due to the efforts of the very keen and efficient staff. There are three very attractive themed pools, one near the entrance with a grassy sunbathing area, a refreshing waterfall and amusing animal figures. The second, deeper pool forms part of the excellent sports complex (with fitness centre, tennis courts, minigolf, crazy golf and football area).

You might like to know

Activities on the beach include windsurfing, sailing, waterskiing, pedaloes and 800 m. from here, sea fishing. The attractive seafront promenade will take you into the centre of Salou.

- ☐ **Beach on site**
- ☑ **Beach within 1 km**
- ☑ **Sandy beach**
- ☑ **Blue Flag quality**
- ☑ **Lifeguard** *(high season)*
- ☑ **Sun lounger and/or deckchair hire**
- ☑ **Watersports** *(e.g. sailing or windsurfing)*
- ☑ **Snacks and drinks**
- ☑ **Sunshades/sunbeds**
- ☐ **Dogs allowed** *(on the beach)*

Facilities: The six clean sanitary blocks have many individual cabins with en-suite facilities. Improvements are made each year. Some blocks have excellent facilities for babies. Launderette with service. Motorcaravan services. Car wash (charged). Gas supplies. Snack bars. Indoor and outdoor restaurants with takeaway. Swimming pools. Fitness centre. Sports complex. Fitness room (charged). Playgrounds including adventure play area. Miniclub. Minigolf. Multiple Internet options including WiFi. Security bracelets. Well equipped medical centre. Off site: Activities on the beach. Bus at gate. Fishing and bicycle hire 100 m. Riding 3 km. Port Aventura 4 km. Resort entertainment. Golf 6 km.

Open: 19 March - 1 November.

Directions: On west side of Salou about 1 km. from the centre, site is well signed from the coast road to Cambrils and from the other town approaches. GPS: 41.075, 1.116

Charges guide

Per unit incl. 2 persons and electricity	€ 27,00 - € 71,00
extra person	€ 6,00
child (4-12 yrs)	€ 4,00

SPAIN – Guardamar del Segura

Camping Marjal

Ctra N332 km 73,4, E-03140 Guardamar del Segura (Alacant)
t: **966 727 070** e: **camping@marjal.com**
alanrogers.com/ES87430 www.campingmarjal.com

Accommodation: ☑ Pitch ☑ Mobile home/chalet ☐ Hotel/B&B ☐ Apartment

Marjal is located beside the estuary of the Segura river, alongside the pine and eucalyptus forests of the Dunas de Guardamar natural park. A fine sandy beach can be reached through the forest (800 m). This is a very smart site with a huge tropical lake-style pool with bar and a superb sports complex. There are 212 pitches on this award-winning site, all with water, electricity, drainage and satellite TV points. The ground is covered with crushed marble, making the pitches clean and pleasant. There is some shade and the site has an open feel with lots of room for manoeuvring. Reception is housed within a delicately coloured building complete with a towering Mirador, topped by a weather vane depicting the 'garza real' (heron) bird which frequents the local area and forms part of the site logo. The large restaurant overlooks the pools and the river that leads to the sea in the near distance. The bar has large terraces fringed by trees, palms and pomegranates.

Special offers

Special discounts available for long stays.

You might like to know

Why not take a day trip to Guardamar del Segura? This typical Spanish town has excellent beaches, a thriving street market and a variety of shops, bars and restaurants.

- ☐ **Beach on site**
- ☑ **Beach within 1 km**
- ☑ **Sandy beach**
- ☑ **Blue Flag quality**
- ☐ **Lifeguard** *(high season)*
- ☐ **Sun lounger and/or deckchair hire**
- ☑ **Watersports** *(e.g. sailing or windsurfing)*
- ☐ **Snacks and drinks**
- ☑ **Sunshades/sunbeds**
- ☐ **Dogs allowed** *(on the beach)*

Facilities: Three excellent heated toilet blocks have free hot water, separators between sinks, spacious showers and some cabins. Each block has high quality facilities for babies and disabled campers, modern laundry and dishwashing rooms. Car wash. Well stocked supermarket. Restaurants. Bar. Large outdoor pool complex (1/6-31/10). Heated indoor pool (low season). Jacuzzi. Sauna. Solarium. Beauty Salon. Superb well equipped gym. Aerobics. Physiotherapy. All activities discounted for campers. Play room. Minigolf. Floodlit tennis/soccer pitch. Bicycle hire. Car rental. Games room. TV room. Full entertainment programme. Hairdresser. ATM. Business centre. Internet access and free WiFi. Off site: Beach 800 m. Riding and golf 4 km. Parc Natural de las Dunas de Guardamar alongside site.

Open: All year.

Directions: On N332 40 km. south of Alicante, site is on the sea side between 73 and 74 km. markers. GPS: 38.10933, -0.65467

Charges guide

Per unit incl. 2 persons and electricity	€ 38,00 - € 65,00
extra person	€ 7,00 - € 9,00
child (4-12 yrs)	€ 5,00 - € 6,00

SPAIN – Noja

Camping Playa Joyel

Playa de Ris, E-39180 Noja (Cantabria)
t: **942 630 081** e: **playajoyel@telefonica.net**
alanrogers.com/ES90000 www.playajoyel.com

Accommodation: ☑ Pitch ☑ Mobile home/chalet ☐ Hotel/B&B ☐ Apartment

This very attractive holiday and touring site is some 40 kilometres from Santander and 80 kilometres from Bilbao. It is a busy, high quality, comprehensively equipped site by a superb beach providing 1,000 well shaded, marked and numbered pitches with 6A electricity available. These include 80 large pitches of 100 sq.m. Some 250 pitches are occupied by tour operators and seasonal units. This well managed site has a lot to offer for family holidays with much going on in high season when it gets crowded. The swimming pool complex (with lifeguard) is free to campers and the superb beaches are cleaned daily mid June to mid September. Two beach exits lead to the main beach where there are some undertows, or if you turn left you will find a reasonably placid estuary. An unusual feature here is the nature park within the site boundary which has a selection of animals to see. This overlooks a protected area of marsh where European birds spend the winter.

You might like to know

The fine sandy beach, which is excellent for surfing, is cleaned daily. Low tide reveals warm pools for younger children and rock pools with small fish and crabs.

- ☑ **Beach on site**
- ☐ **Beach within 1 km**
- ☑ **Sandy beach**
- ☐ **Blue Flag quality**
- ☐ **Lifeguard** *(high season)*
- ☐ **Sun lounger and/or deckchair hire**
- ☑ **Watersports** *(e.g. sailing or windsurfing)*
- ☐ **Snacks and drinks**
- ☐ **Sunshades/sunbeds**
- ☐ **Dogs allowed** *(on the beach)*

Facilities: Six excellent, spacious and fully equipped toilet blocks include baby baths. Large laundry. Motorcaravan services. Gas supplies. Freezer service. Supermarket (all season). Shop. Kiosk. Restaurant and takeaway (1/7-31/8). Bar and snacks. Swimming pools, bathing caps compulsory (20/5-15/9). Entertainment organised with soundproofed pub/disco (July/Aug). Gym park. Tennis. Playground. Riding. Fishing. Animal park. Hairdresser (July/Aug). Medical centre. Torches necessary in some areas. Animals are not accepted. Off site: Bicycle hire and large sports complex with indoor pool 1 km. Sailing and boat launching 10 km. Golf 20 km.

Open: 15 April - 1 October.

Directions: From A8 (Bilbao - Santander) take km. 185 exit and N634 towards Beranga. Almost immediately turn right on CA147 to Noja. In 10 km. turn left at multiple campsite signs and go through town. At beach follow signs to site. GPS: 43.48948, -3.53700

Charges guide

Per unit incl. 2 persons and electricity	€ 28,20 - € 47,40
extra person	€ 4,40 - € 6,70
child (3-9 yrs)	€ 3,10 - € 5,00

PORTUGAL – São Pedro de Moel

Orbitur São Pedro de Moel

Rua Volta do Sete, P-2430 São Pedro de Moel (Leiria)
t: **244 599 168** e: **infospedro@orbitur.pt**
alanrogers.com/PO8100 www.orbitur.pt

Accommodation: ☑ Pitch ☑ Mobile home/chalet ☐ Hotel/B&B ☐ Apartment

This quiet and very attractive site is situated under tall pines, on the edge of the rather select, small resort of São Pedro de Moel. This is a shady site which can be crowded in July and August. The 525 pitches are in blocks and unmarked (cars may be parked separately) with 404 electrical connections. A few pitches are used for permanent units. Although there are areas of soft sand, there should be no problem in finding a firm place. The large restaurant and bar are modern as is the superb swimming pool, paddling pool and flume (there is a lifeguard). The attractive, sandy beach is about 600 m. walk downhill from the site (you can take the car, although parking may be difficult in the town) and is sheltered from the wind by low cliffs.

You might like to know

The sheltered beach is only 600 m. from the campsite.

- ☐ **Beach on site**
- ☑ **Beach within 1 km**
- ☑ **Sandy beach**
- ☐ **Blue Flag quality**
- ☐ **Lifeguard** *(high season)*
- ☐ **Sun lounger and/or deckchair hire**
- ☑ **Watersports** *(e.g. sailing or windsurfing)*
- ☑ **Snacks and drinks**
- ☑ **Sunshades/sunbeds**
- ☐ **Dogs allowed** *(on the beach)*

Facilities: Four clean toilet blocks have mainly British style toilets (some with bidets), some washbasins with hot water. Hot showers are mostly in one unisex block. Laundry. Motorcaravan services. Gas supplies. Supermarket. Large restaurant and bar with terrace (closed in November). Swimming pools (1/3-30/9). Satellite TV. Games room. Playground. Tennis. WiFi. Off site: Bus service 100 m. Beach 500 m. Fishing 1 km.

Open: All year.

Directions: Site is 9 km. west of Marinha Grande, on the right as you enter São Pedro de Moel. GPS: 39.75883, -9.02229

Charges guide

Per person	€ 5,10
child (5-10 yrs)	€ 2,60
pitch	€ 10,90 - € 11,90
electricity	€ 2,90 - € 3,50

PORTUGAL – Lagos

Camping Turiscampo

N125, Espiche, Luz, P-8600 Lagos (Faro)
t: 282 789 265 e: info@turiscampo.com
alanrogers.com/PO8202 www.turiscampo.com

Accommodation: ☑ Pitch ☑ Mobile home/chalet ☐ Hotel/B&B ☐ Apartment

This good quality site has been thoughtfully refurbished and updated since it was purchased by the friendly Coll family, who are known to us from their previous Spanish site. The site provides 206 pitches for touring units, mainly in rows of terraces, all with electricity (6/10A) and some with shade. Twelve pitches have water and waste water. The pitches vary in size (70-120 sq.m). The upper areas of the site are mainly used for bungalow accommodation (and are generally separate from the touring areas). A new, elevated Californian style pool plus a children's pool have been constructed. The supporting structure is a water cascade and surround, and a large sun lounger area on astroturf. One side of the pool area is open to the road. The restaurant/bar has been tastefully refurbished and Roberto and his staff are delighted to use their excellent English, providing good fare at most reasonable prices. The restaurant has two patios, one is used for live entertainment and discos in season and the other for dining out.

You might like to know

The campsite is 4 km. from Lagos and a little further is Portimão, both with superb sandy beaches.

- ☐ Beach on site
- ☑ Beach within 1 km
- ☑ Sandy beach
- ☐ Blue Flag quality
- ☐ Lifeguard *(high season)*
- ☐ Sun lounger and/or deckchair hire
- ☑ Watersports *(e.g. sailing or windsurfing)*
- ☑ Snacks and drinks
- ☐ Sunshades/sunbeds
- ☐ Dogs allowed *(on the beach)*

Facilities: Four toilet blocks are well located around the site. Two have been refurbished, two are new and contain modern facilities for disabled campers. Hot water throughout. Facilities for children. Washing machines. Shop. Gas supplies. Restaurant/bar. Swimming pool (Mar-Oct) with two terraces. Bicycle hire. Entertainment in high season on the bar terrace. Two playgrounds. Adult art workshops. Aqua gymnastics. Miniclub (5-12 yrs) in season. Boules. Archery. Sports field. Cable TV. Internet. WiFi on payment. Bungalows to rent. Off site: Bus to Lagos and other towns from Praia da Luz village 1.5 km. Fishing and beach 2 km. Golf 4 km. Sailing and boat launching 5 km. Riding 10 km.

Open: All year.

Directions: Take exit 1 from the N125 Lagos - Vila do Bispo. The impressive entrance is about 3 km. on the right. GPS: 37.10111, -8.73278

Charges guide

Per unit incl. 2 persons and electricity	€ 16,20 - € 28,83
extra person	€ 3,28 - € 6,56
child (3-10 yrs)	€ 1,77 - € 3,28
dog	€ 1,01

Orbitur Camping Quarteira

Estrada da Fonte Santa, avenida Sá Cameiro, P-8125-618 Quarteira (Faro)
t: **289 302 826** e: **infoquarteira@orbitur.pt**
alanrogers.com/PO8220 www.orbitur.pt

Accommodation: ☑ Pitch ☑ Mobile home/chalet ☐ Hotel/B&B ☐ Apartment

This is a large, busy, attractive site on undulating ground with some terracing, taking 795 units. On the outskirts of the popular Algarve resort of Quarteira, it is 600 m. from a sandy beach which stretches for about a kilometre to the town centre. Many of the unmarked pitches have shade from tall trees and there are a few small, individual pitches of 50 sq.m. with electricity and water. There are 659 electrical connections. Like others along this coast, the site encourages long winter stays. There is a large restaurant and supermarket which have a separate entrance for local trade. The swimming pools (free for campers) are excellent, featuring pools for adults (with a large flume) and children (with fountains).

You might like to know

The city of Faro is a bus ride away – the bus leaves from outside the campsite gate; alternatively visit Almancil and the São Lourenço Church.

- ☐ **Beach on site**
- ☑ **Beach within 1 km**
- ☑ **Sandy beach**
- ☐ **Blue Flag quality**
- ☐ **Lifeguard** *(high season)*
- ☑ **Sun lounger and/or deckchair hire**
- ☑ **Watersports** *(e.g. sailing or windsurfing)*
- ☑ **Snacks and drinks**
- ☑ **Sunshades/sunbeds**
- ☐ **Dogs allowed** *(on the beach)*

Facilities: Five toilet blocks provide British and Turkish style toilets, washbasins with cold water, hot showers plus facilities for disabled visitors. Washing machines. Motorcaravan services. Gas supplies. Supermarket. Self-service restaurant (closed Nov). Separate takeaway (from late May). Swimming pools (Apr-Sept). Room with bar and satellite TV. WiFi. Tennis. Open-air disco (high season). Off site: Bus from gate to Faro. Fishing and bicycle hire (summer) 1 km. Golf 4 km.

Open: All year.

Directions: Turn off N125 for village of Almancil. In the village take road south to Quarteira. Site is on the left 1 km. after large, official town welcome sign. GPS: 37.06666, -8.08333

Charges guide

Per person	€ 5,90
child (5-10 yrs)	€ 3,00
pitch	€ 12,70 - € 13,70
electricity	€ 2,90 - € 3,50

ITALY – Grado

Camping Tenuta Primero

Via Monfalcone 14, I-34073 Grado (Friuli - Venézia Giúlia)
t: 043 189 6900 e: info@tenuta-primero.com
alanrogers.com/IT60065 www.tenuta-primero.com

Accommodation: ☑ Pitch ☑ Mobile home/chalet ☐ Hotel/B&B ☐ Apartment

Tenuta Primero is a large, attractive, well run, family owned site with direct access to its own private beach via a pathway on top of a low bank. Apart from the beach – an ideal place to enjoy the view, sunbathe or take a dip in the Adriatic – the site offers a wealth of facilities and activities catering for all members of the family. The 740 pitches are all level, with 6A electricity, some separating hedges and ample tree shade, and many are reached by branch roads from an attractive palm tree-lined avenue. The site does not accept dogs. The site has several restaurants and bars conveniently tucked around the site; the large flower decked Terrazza Mare overlooking the sea is particularly attractive. As well as the many activities that the site has to offer, its location makes it a useful base to visit many of the historically interesting towns and sites in the region. It's a good point to stop over, relax and stock up on the way down to Croatia or Slovenia, however be prepared to spend a bit more time than planned to enjoy everything on offer here.

You might like to know

If you feel like a change from the beach, why not take a day trip to Venice?

- ☑ Beach on site
- ☐ Beach within 1 km
- ☑ Sandy beach
- ☑ Blue Flag quality
- ☑ Lifeguard *(high season)*
- ☑ Sun lounger and/or deckchair hire
- ☑ Watersports *(e.g. sailing or windsurfing)*
- ☑ Snacks and drinks
- ☑ Sunshades/sunbeds
- ☐ Dogs allowed *(on the beach)*

Facilities: Nine well maintained sanitary blocks, seven with facilities for disabled visitors. Washing machines and dryers. Motorcaravan service point. Swimming pools and paddling pool. Shop. Bars and restaurants, pizzeria (all April-Sept), takeaway (May-Sept). Beauty salon. Aerobics. Water gymnastics. Football pitch. Tennis courts. Children's playgrounds. Windsurfing. Marina, sailing, boat launching and boat hire. Bicycle hire. Children's and family entertainment. Live music, disco, dancing. Private beach with sunshades, deck chairs and jetty. Internet corner and WiFi (charged). Off site: 18-hole golf course opposite entrance. Grado 5 km. Riding 7 km. Venice. Palmanova. Aquileia with mosaic floors.

Open: 1 April - 3 October.

Directions: Leave the A4 autostrada at the Palmanova exit and head towards Grado. In Grado, after crossing the causeway turn left towards Monfalcone on the SP19. Site is on the right after 5 km. opposite a large golf course. GPS: 45.7051, 13.4640

Charges guide

Per unit incl. 2 persons and electricity	€ 19,00 - € 49,00
extra person	€ 6,00 - € 12,00
child (0-15 yrs)	free - € 10,00

ITALY – Cavallino-Treporti

Camping Union Lido Vacanze

Via Fausta 258, I-30013 Cavallino-Treporti (Veneto)
t: **041 257 5111** e: **info@unionlido.com**
alanrogers.com/IT60200 www.unionlido.com

Accommodation: ☑ Pitch ☑ Mobile home/chalet ☑ Hotel/B&B ☑ Apartment

This amazing site is very large, offering everything a camper could wish for. It is extremely well organised and it has been said to set the standard that others follow. It lies right beside the sea with direct access to a 1.2 km. long, broad sandy beach which shelves very gradually and provides very safe bathing (there are lifeguards). The site itself is regularly laid out with parallel access roads under a covering of poplars, pine and other trees providing good shade. There are 2,222 pitches for touring units, all with 6/10A electricity and 1,777 also have water and drainage. Because of the size of the site there is an internal road train and amenities are repeated across the site (cycling is not permitted and cars are parked away from the pitches). You really would not need to leave this site – everything is here, including a sophisticated wellness centre. Overnight parking is provided outside the gate with electricity, toilets and showers for those arriving after 21.00. There are two aqua parks, one with fine sandy beaches.

You might like to know

One of Europe's largest sites, looking straight out to the Adriatic with a long private beach (1,200 metres), Union Lido is a top quality holiday centre with a wide range of amenities.

- ☑ **Beach on site**
- ☐ **Beach within 1 km**
- ☑ **Sandy beach**
- ☑ **Blue Flag quality**
- ☑ **Lifeguard** *(high season)*
- ☑ **Sun lounger and/or deckchair hire**
- ☑ **Watersports** *(e.g. sailing or windsurfing)*
- ☑ **Snacks and drinks**
- ☑ **Sunshades/sunbeds**
- ☐ **Dogs allowed** *(on the beach)*

Facilities: Fourteen well kept, fully equipped toilet blocks which open and close progressively during the season; 11 have facilities for disabled visitors. Launderette. Motorcaravan service points. Gas supplies. Comprehensive shopping areas (open late). Eight restaurants each with a different style plus 11 pleasant and lively bars (open all season). Impressive aqua parks (all season). Tennis. Riding. Minigolf. Skating. Bicycle hire. Archery. Two fitness tracks in 4 ha. natural park with play area and supervised play for children. Golf academy. Diving centre and school. Windsurfing school in season. Boat excursions. Recreational events. Hairdressers. Internet cafés. ATM. Dogs are not accepted. Off site: Boat launching 3.5 km. Aqualandia (special rates).

Open: 22 April - 25 September (with all services).

Directions: From Venice - Trieste autostrada leave at exit for airport or Quarto d'Altino and follow signs first for Jesolo and then Punta Sabbioni, and site will be seen just after Cavallino on the left. GPS: 45.467883, 12.530367

Charges guide

Per unit incl. 2 persons and electricity	€ 25,40 - € 47,50
extra person	€ 6,60 - € 11,20
child (1-11 yrs)	€ 3,70 - € 9,30

ITALY – Cavallino-Treporti

Camping Village Garden Paradiso

Via Baracca 55, I-30013 Cavallino-Treporti (Veneto)
t: 041 968 075 e: info@gardenparadiso.it
alanrogers.com/IT60400 www.gardenparadiso.it

Accommodation: ☑ Pitch ☑ Mobile home/chalet ☐ Hotel/B&B ☐ Apartment

There are many sites in this area and there is much competition in providing a range of facilities. Garden Paradiso is a good seaside site which also provides three excellent, centrally situated pools, a fitness centre, minigolf, a train to the market and other activities for children. Compared with other sites here, this one is of medium size with 776 pitches. All have electricity (4/6A), water and drainage points and all are marked and numbered with hard access roads, under a good cover of trees. Many flowers and shrubs give a pleasant and peaceful appearance and a new reception provides a professional welcome. The restaurant, with self-service at lunch time and waiter service at night, is near the beach with a bar/snack bar in the centre of the site. The site is directly on the sea with a beach of fine sand. A community bus service runs daily to the local markets. Used by tour operators (35 pitches).

You might like to know

The fine sandy beach slopes gently down to the sea and twice a week the pirate ship, Jolly Roger, sails from here. There are children's slides and swings and beach volleyball.

- ☑ Beach on site
- ☑ Beach within 1 km
- ☑ Sandy beach
- ☐ Blue Flag quality
- ☑ Lifeguard *(high season)*
- ☑ Sun lounger and/or deckchair hire
- ☑ Watersports *(e.g. sailing or windsurfing)*
- ☑ Snacks and drinks
- ☑ Sunshades/sunbeds
- ☐ Dogs allowed *(on the beach)*

Facilities: Four brick toilet blocks are tiled and fully equipped with a mix of British and Turkish style toilets. Facilities for babies. Washing machines and dryers. Motorcaravan services. Shopping complex. Restaurant (23/4-30/9). Snack bar and takeaway. 'Aqualandia' pool complex (charged). Fitness centre. Tennis. Minigolf. Play area. Organised entertainment and excursions (high season). Bicycle hire. WiFi. Dogs are not accepted. Off site: Riding 2 km. Fishing 2.5 km.

Open: 23 April - 30 September.

Directions: Leave Venice - Trieste autostrada either by taking airport or Quarto d'Altino exits; follow signs to Jesolo and Punta Sabbioni. Take first road left after Cavallino roundabout and site is a little way on the right.
GPS: 45.47897, 12.56359

Charges guide

Per unit incl. 2 persons, electricity, water and drain	€ 20,10 - € 43,20
extra person	€ 4,80 - € 9,50
child (6-12 yrs) or senior (over 61 yrs)	€ 3,25 - € 7,30
child (3-5 yrs)	free - € 6,30

ITALY – Cavallino-Treporti

Camping Village Europa

Via Fausta 332, I-30013 Cavallino-Treporti (Veneto)
t: **041 968 069** e: **info@campingeuropa.com**
alanrogers.com/IT60410 www.campingeuropa.com

Accommodation: ☑ Pitch ☑ Mobile home/chalet ☐ Hotel/B&B ☑ Apartment

Europa is a large site in a great position with direct access to a fine sandy Blue Flag beach with lifeguards. There are 500 touring pitches, 450 of which have 8A electricity, water, drainage and satellite TV connections. There is a separate area for campers with dogs and some smaller pitches are available for those with tents. The site is kept beautifully clean and neat and there is an impressive array of restaurants, bars, shops and leisure amenities. These are cleverly laid out along an avenue and include a jeweller's, a doctor's surgery, Internet services and much more. Leisure facilities are arranged around the site. The touring area is surprisingly peaceful for a site of this size. A professional team provides entertainment and regular themed summer events. Some restaurant tables have pleasant sea views. Venice is easily accessible by bus and then ferry from Punta Sabbioni.

You might like to know

The long wide beach of very fine sand is cleaned daily. It features natural dunes and is ideal for young children.

- ☑ **Beach on site**
- ☐ **Beach within 1 km**
- ☑ **Sandy beach**
- ☑ **Blue Flag quality**
- ☑ **Lifeguard** *(high season)*
- ☑ **Sun lounger and/or deckchair hire**
- ☑ **Watersports** *(e.g. sailing or windsurfing)*
- ☑ **Snacks and drinks**
- ☑ **Sunshades/sunbeds**
- ☐ **Dogs allowed** *(on the beach)*

Facilities: Three superb toilet blocks are kept pristine and have hot water throughout. Facilities for disabled visitors. Washing machines. Large supermarket and shopping centre, bars, restaurants, cafés and pizzeria (all season; takeaway service 15/5-30/9). Excellent pool complex with slide and spa centre (9/4-25/9). Tennis. Games room. Playground. Children's clubs. Entertainment programme. WiFi (charged). Direct access to the beach. Windsurf and pedalo hire. Mobile homes, chalets and 14 eco apartments for rent. Off site: ATM 500 m. Riding and boat launching 1 km. Golf and fishing 4 km. Walking and cycling trails. Excursions to Venice.

Open: 31 March - 30 September.

Directions: From A4 autostrada (approaching from Milan) take Mestre exit and follow signs initially for Venice airport and then Jesolo. From Jesolo, follow signs to Cavallino from where site is well signed. GPS: 45.47380, 12.54903

Charges guide

Per unit incl. 2 persons and electricity	€ 20,00 - € 48,00
extra person	€ 5,00 - € 10,50
child (2-5 yrs)	€ 3,35 - € 9,30

ITALY – Punta Sabbioni

Camping Marina di Venezia

Via Montello 6, I-30013 Punta Sabbioni (Veneto)
t: **041 530 2511** e: **camping@marinadivenezia.it**
alanrogers.com/IT60450 www.marinadivenezia.it

Accommodation: ☑ Pitch ☑ Mobile home/chalet ☐ Hotel/B&B ☐ Apartment

This is a very large site (2,853 pitches) with much the same atmosphere as many other large sites along this appealing stretch of coastline. Marina di Venezia, however, has the advantage of being within walking distance of the ferry to Venice. It will appeal particularly to those who enjoy an extensive range of entertainment and activities, and a lively atmosphere. Individual pitches are marked out on sandy or grassy ground, most separated by trees or hedges. They are of an average size for the region (around 80 sq.m) and all are equipped with electricity and water. The site's excellent sandy beach is one of the widest along this stretch of coast and has five pleasant beach bars. The main pool is Olympic size and there is also a very large children's pool adjacent. The magnificent Aqua Marina Park swimming pool complex is now open and offers amazing amenities (free to all campers). This is a well run site with committed management and staff.

You might like to know

The coast features natural sand dunes, golden sands and safe bathing. There are well-trained and equipped lifeguards, and deckchairs and beach umbrellas for hire. Numerous sporting activities are held including beach volleyball, beach football, bowls, surfing, kite-surfing, stand up paddling, windsurfing, canoing, sailing and pedaloes.

- ☑ **Beach on site**
- ☐ **Beach within 1 km**
- ☑ **Sandy beach**
- ☑ **Blue Flag quality**
- ☑ **Lifeguard** *(high season)*
- ☑ **Sun lounger and/or deckchair hire**
- ☑ **Watersports** *(e.g. sailing or windsurfing)*
- ☑ **Snacks and drinks**
- ☐ **Sunshades/sunbeds**
- ☐ **Dogs allowed** *(on the beach)*

Facilities: Ten modern toilet blocks (two recently replaced by a new one) are maintained to a high standard with good hot showers and a reasonable proportion of British style toilets. Good provision for disabled visitors. Washing machines and dryers. Range of shops. Several bars, restaurants and takeaways. Swimming pool complex with slides and flumes. Several play areas. Tennis. Windsurf and catamaran hire. Kite hire. Wide range of organised entertainment. WiFi Internet access in all bars and cafés. Church. Special area and facilities for dog owners.

Open: 16 April - 30 September.

Directions: From A4 motorway, take Jesolo exit. After Jesolo continue towards Punta Sabbioni. Site is clearly signed to the left towards the end of this road, close to the Venice ferries.
GPS: 45.43750, 12.43805

Charges guide

Per unit incl. 2 persons and electricity	€ 19,80 - € 48,90
extra person	€ 4,40 - € 9,90
child (2-5 yrs) or senior (60+)	€ 3,70 - € 8,00
dog	€ 1,10 - € 3,50

ITALY – Sottomarina di Chioggia

Camping Village Oasi

Via A Barbarigo 147, I-30015 Sottomarina di Chioggia (Veneto)
t: **041 554 1145** e: **info@campingoasi.com**
alanrogers.com/IT60540 www.campingoasi.com

Accommodation: ☑ Pitch ☑ Mobile home/chalet ☐ Hotel/B&B ☐ Apartment

Camping Oasi is a traditional, friendly, family site where many Italian families return for the summer – you could certainly practise your Italian language skills here. The Tiozzi family will make you feel very welcome. The flat, grass pitches for tourers are in separate areas from the permanent units, some being near the playground and football area. Varying in size (65-80 sq.m) with a choice of shade or sun, all have 6A electricity, 100 have water and drainage. There is a harbour wall walk to the private soft sand beach where a new second bar and restaurant provides drinks, snacks and meals. The touring pitches are near the beach access and some have views of the river leading to the sea. The site has two restaurants – try the excellent seafood! An entertainment team works with children through the day in high season, culminating in a show outside the restaurant in the evening. We recommend a bicycle trip to the ancient fishing city of Chioggia. It resembles a mini-Venice with its narrow streets and canals.

You might like to know

The new restaurant here features Venetian specialities and seafood. Enjoy an apéritif at sunset, with live music.

- ☑ **Beach on site**
- ☐ **Beach within 1 km**
- ☑ **Sandy beach**
- ☐ **Blue Flag quality**
- ☑ **Lifeguard** *(high season)*
- ☑ **Sun lounger and/or deckchair hire**
- ☑ **Watersports** *(e.g. sailing or windsurfing)*
- ☑ **Snacks and drinks**
- ☑ **Sunshades/sunbeds**
- ☐ **Dogs allowed** *(on the beach)*

Facilities: Two good sanitary blocks with mostly British style toilets and free hot showers. There are good facilities for disabled visitors and for children and babies (both some way from the furthest touring pitches). Pleasant swimming pool and paddling pool with flumes (a hoist is available allowing easier access for disabled visitors into the swimming pool). Multisport pitch. Adventure play area. Tennis. Bicycle hire. Watersports. Fishing. Riding. WiFi (charged). Communal barbecue area. Off site: Historical city of Chioggia. ATM 2 km.

Open: 25 March - 30 September.

Directions: Site is off the S309 south of Chioggia. Follow signs to Sottomarina, crossing Laguna del Lusenzo, then look for site signs. Site off this road (Viale Mediterraneo) to the right. It is the last along this narrow road.
GPS: 45.18148, 12.30755

Charges guide

Per unit incl. 2 persons and electricity	€ 20,10 - € 35,10
extra person	€ 5,40 - € 8,30
child (1-5 yrs)	€ 2,60 - € 4,40
dog	€ 2,70 - € 3,70

ITALY – Levico Terme

Camping Lago di Levico

Loc. Pleina 5, I-38056 Levico Terme (Trentino - Alto Adige)
t: 046 170 6491 e: info@lagolevico.com
alanrogers.com/IT62290 www.lagolevico.com

Accommodation: ☑ Pitch ☑ Mobile home/chalet ☐ Hotel/B&B ☐ Apartment

Camping Lago di Levico, by a pretty lakeside in the mountains, is the merger of two popular sites, Camping Lévico and Camping Jolly. Brothers Andrea and Geno Antoniolli are making great improvements, already there is an impressive new reception and further developments of the lakeside and swimming areas are planned. The lakeside pitches are quite special. There are 430 mostly grassy and shaded pitches (70-120 sq.m) with 6A electricity, 150 also have water and drainage and 12 have private facilities. Staff are welcoming and fluent in English. The swimming pool complex is popular, as is the summer family entertainment. There is a small supermarket on site and it is a short distance to the local village. The restaurant, bar, pizzeria and takeaway are open all season. The beautiful grass shores of the lake are ideal for sunbathing and the crystal clear water is ideal for enjoying (non-motorised) water activities. This is a site where the natural beauty of an Italian lake can be enjoyed without excessive commercial tourism.

You might like to know

There is a large private beach, but the clear, shallow waters of the lake offer opportunities for swimming, fishing, canoeing, and boating. Canoes and pedaloes can be hired from reception.

- ☑ Beach on site
- ☐ Beach within 1 km
- ☐ Sandy beach
- ☑ Blue Flag quality
- ☑ Lifeguard *(high season)*
- ☑ Sun lounger and/or deckchair hire
- ☑ Watersports *(e.g. sailing or windsurfing)*
- ☑ Snacks and drinks
- ☑ Sunshades/sunbeds
- ☐ Dogs allowed *(on the beach)*

Facilities: Four modern sanitary blocks provide hot water for showers, washbasins and washing. Mostly British style toilets. Single locked unit for disabled visitors. Laundry facilities. Freezer. Motorcaravan service point. Good shop. Bar/restaurant and takeaway. Outdoor swimming pool. Play area. Miniclub and entertainment (high season). Fishing. Satellite TV and cartoon cinema. Internet access (free in low season). Kayak hire. Tennis. Torches useful. Off site: Boat launching 500 m. Bicycle hire and bicycle track 1.5 km. Town with all the usual facilities and ATM 2 km. Riding 3 km. Golf 6 km.

Open: 15 April - 10 October.

Directions: From A22 Verona - Bolzano road take turn for Trento on S47 to Levico Terme where campsite is very well signed.
GPS: 46.00799, 11.28454

Charges guide

Per unit incl. 2 persons and electricity	€ 9,50 - € 38,00
extra person	€ 3,00 - € 14,25
child (3-11 yrs)	free - € 6,50
dog	free - € 5,00

ITALY – San Remo

Camping Villaggio dei Fiori

Via Tiro a Volo 3, I-18038 San Remo (Ligúria)
t: **018 466 0635** e: **info@villaggiodeifiori.it**
alanrogers.com/IT64010 www.villaggiodeifiori.it

Accommodation: ☑ Pitch ☑ Mobile home/chalet ☐ Hotel/B&B ☐ Apartment

Open all year round, this open and spacious site is a member of the Senelia group and maintains very high standards. It is ideal for exploring the Italian and French Rivieras or for just relaxing by the enjoyable, filtered sea water pools or on the private beach. Unusually, all of the pitch areas at the site are totally paved, with some extremely large pitches for large units (ask reception to open another gate for entry). Electricity (3/6A) is available (at extra cost) to all 107 pitches; 20 also have water and drainage, and there is an outside sink and cold water for every four pitches. There is ample shade from mature trees and shrubs, which are constantly watered and cared for in summer. The 'gold' pitches and some wonderful tent pitches are along the seafront with great views. There is a path to a secluded and pleasant beach with sparkling waters, overlooked by a large patio area. The rocky surrounds are excellent for snorkelling and fishing, with ladder access to the water. The friendly management speak excellent English.

You might like to know

A new cycle track is being developed along the seafront, following the tracks of a former railway.

- ☑ **Beach on site**
- ☐ **Beach within 1 km**
- ☑ **Sandy beach**
- ☐ **Blue Flag quality**
- ☐ **Lifeguard** *(high season)*
- ☑ **Sun lounger and/or deckchair hire**
- ☐ **Watersports** *(e.g. sailing or windsurfing)*
- ☐ **Snacks and drinks**
- ☐ **Sunshades/sunbeds**
- ☐ **Dogs allowed** *(on the beach)*

Facilities: Four clean and modern toilet blocks have British and Turkish style WCs and hot water throughout. Controllable showers. Baby rooms. Facilities for disabled campers. Laundry facilities. Motorcaravan services. Gas. Bar sells limited essential supplies. Large restaurant. Pizzeria and takeaway (all year; prepaid card system). Sea water swimming pools (small extra charge in high season) and heated whirlpool spa (June-Sept). Tennis. Excellent play area. Fishing. Satellite TV. Internet access. WiFi (charged). Bicycle hire. Dogs are not accepted. Off site: Bus at gate. Supermarket 100 m. Shop 150 m. Riding and golf 2 km. Very safe cycle route to the city and a further 24 km. along coastal path.

Open: All year.

Directions: From SS1 (Ventimiglia - Imperia), site is on right just before San Remo. There is a very sharp right turn into site if approaching from the west. From autostrada A10 take San Remo exit. Site is well signed. GPS: 43.80117, 7.74867

Charges guide

Per unit incl. 4 persons and electricity	€ 35,00 - € 72,00

Some charges must be paid on arrival.

ITALY – Ceriale

Camping Baciccia

Via Torino 19, I-17023 Ceriale (Ligúria)
t: 018 299 0743 e: info@campingbaciccia.it
alanrogers.com/IT64030 www.campingbaciccia.it

Accommodation: ☑ Pitch ☑ Mobile home/chalet ☐ Hotel/B&B ☐ Apartment

This friendly, family run site is a popular holiday destination. Baciccia was the nickname of the present owner's grandfather who grew fruit trees and tomatoes on the site. Tall eucalyptus trees shade the 106 flat pitches which encircle the central facilities block. The pitches are on flat ground and all have electricity. There is always a family member by the gate to greet you, and Vincenzina and Giovanni, along with their daughter and son, Laura and Mauro, work tirelessly to ensure that you enjoy your stay. The pool has a giant elephant slide and there is a vibrant play area for children. The informal restaurant serves delightful seasonal Italian dishes and overlooks a large swimming pool. There is a free shuttle to the site's private beach and the town has the usual seaside attractions. This site will suit campers looking for a family atmosphere with none of the brashness of large seaside sites. If you have forgotten anything by way of camping equipment just ask and the family will lend it to you.

Special offers

Contact site for details of special low-season offers.

You might like to know

Baciccia is just 500 m. from the free beach, and 1.5 km. from the private beach (free shuttle bus).

- ☐ Beach on site
- ☑ Beach within 1 km
- ☑ Sandy beach
- ☑ Blue Flag quality
- ☑ Lifeguard *(high season)*
- ☑ Sun lounger and/or deckchair hire
- ☑ Watersports *(e.g. sailing or windsurfing)*
- ☑ Snacks and drinks
- ☑ Sunshades/sunbeds
- ☐ Dogs allowed *(on the beach)*

Facilities: Two clean and modern sanitary blocks near reception have British and Turkish style WCs and hot water throughout. Laundry. Motorcaravan services. Restaurant/bar. Shop. Pizzeria and takeaway. Swimming pool and paddling pool (1/4-31/10) and private beach. Tennis. Bowls. Excellent new play area. Bicycle hire. Wood-burning stove and barbecue. WiFi. Fishing. Diving. Entertainment for children and adults in high season. Excursions.
Off site: Department store 150 m. Bus 200 m. Aquapark 500 m. Riding and golf 2 km. Ancient town of Albenga (2,000 years old) 3 km. Parachuting school 10 km.

Open: 20 March - 3 November, 4 December - 10 January.

Directions: From the A10 between Imperia and Savona, take Albenga exit. Follow signs Ceriale/Savona and Aquapark Caravelle (which is 500 m. from site) and then site signs. Site is just south of Savona. GPS: 44.08165, 8.21763

Charges guide

Per unit incl. 3 persons (over 2 yrs) and electricity	€ 26,50 - € 49,00
extra person	€ 6,50 - € 11,00
dog	€ 2,50 - € 5,00

ITALY – Savignano Mare

Camping Villaggio Rubicone

Via Matrice Destra 1, I-47039 Savignano Mare (Emília-Romagna)
t: **054 134 6377** e: **info@campingrubicone.com**
alanrogers.com/IT66240 www.campingrubicone.com

Accommodation: ☑ Pitch ☑ Mobile home/chalet ☐ Hotel/B&B ☐ Apartment

This is a sophisticated, professionally run site where the friendly owners, Sandro and Paolo Grotti are keen to fulfill your every need. Rubicone covers over 30 acres of thoughtfully landscaped, level ground by the sea. There is an amazing array of amenities on offer. The 457 touring pitches vary in size (up to 100 sq.m) and are arranged in back to back, double rows. In some areas the central pitches are a little tight for manoeuvring larger units. All the pitches are kept very neat with hedges and all have electricity, 150 with water and drainage and 20 with private sanitary facilities. Some are shaded by poplar trees. There are many bars around the site, from beach bars to night club bars and the restaurant offers excellent food and efficient service at very reasonable prices. The animation programme is for both young and old and is staged in a circular terraced area near the main bar. Across the railway line (via an underpass) is a huge complex including excellent swimming pools for adults and children.

Special offers

Free courses in sailing and canoeing.

You might like to know

A first rate, 4 star holiday resort directly on the seafront with a private beach and free umbrellas, a rare opportunity on the Adriatic coast.

☑ **Beach on site**
☐ **Beach within 1 km**
☑ **Sandy beach**
☐ **Blue Flag quality**
☑ **Lifeguard** *(high season)*
☑ **Sun lounger and/or deckchair hire**
☑ **Watersports**
(e.g. sailing or windsurfing)
☑ **Snacks and drinks**
☑ **Sunshades/sunbeds**
☐ **Dogs allowed** *(on the beach)*

Facilities: Modern heated toilet blocks have hot water for showers and washbasins, mainly British style toilets, baby rooms and two excellent units for disabled visitors. Washing machines. Motorcaravan services. Excellent shop and bars (21/5-18/9). Restaurant, snack bar and pizzeria (28/5-11/9). Swimming pools (21/5-18/9; caps compulsory). Games room with internet access. Golf (lessons available). Tennis. Solarium. Jacuzzi. Beach with lifeguard. Fishing. Sailing/windsurfing schools. Dogs are not accepted. Off site: Bicycle hire 500 m. Riding 2 km. Golf 15 km. Cesenatico 5 km. Rimini 12 km. Riccione 25 km.

Open: 21 May - 18 September.

Directions: Site is 12 km. northwest of Rimini. From Bologna (autostrada A14) exit Rimini Nord. Continue on SS16 'Adriatica' direction Ravenna, then exit Savignano Mare. At the roundabout go straight through to San Mauro Mare and turn left immediately after the railway. At the end of the street turn right and you have arrived at Camping Rubicone. GPS: 44.16475, 12.441117

Charges guide

Per unit incl. 2 persons and electricity	€ 22,90 - € 41,90

No credit cards.

ITALY – Martinsicuro

Camping Village Duca Amedeo

Lungomare Europa, 158, I-64014 Martinsicuro (Abruzzo)
t: **086 179 7376** e: **info@ducaamedeo.it**
alanrogers.com/IT67982 www.ducaamedeo.it

Accommodation: ☑ Pitch ☑ Mobile home/chalet ☐ Hotel/B&B ☐ Apartment

Duca Amadeo is in an attractive setting with direct access to a broad, sandy beach. The beach shelves very gradually and is ideal for younger children. This site also enjoys the advantage of being set well back from the busy coastal railway line. There are 149 pitches here, of which 55 are available to tourers. These are of a reasonable size and most have electrical connections. There are also a number of chalets and wood-clad mobile homes for rent. Leisure facilities include an attractive swimming pool, with a wide sun terrace. The site is lively in high season with a programme of activities for all the family. The resort town of Martinsicuro is within walking distance and is a lovely place to explore, located at the mouth of the river Tronto. The town has a Roman history and the 16th-century Charles V Tower houses an interesting archaeological museum. Further afield, the Abruzzo National Park merits exploration and fulfils an important conservation role in maintaining the habitat of the Italian wolf and Marsican brown bear.

You might like to know

The town centre can be easily reached on foot and has a wonderful selection of tempting ice cream parlours!

- ☑ **Beach on site**
- ☐ **Beach within 1 km**
- ☑ **Sandy beach**
- ☑ **Blue Flag quality**
- ☑ **Lifeguard** *(high season)*
- ☑ **Sun lounger and/or deckchair hire**
- ☑ **Watersports** *(e.g. sailing or windsurfing)*
- ☐ **Snacks and drinks**
- ☑ **Sunshades/sunbeds**
- ☐ **Dogs allowed** *(on the beach)*

Facilities: Swimming pool (with sun terrace and children's pool). Picnic area. Games room. Children's playground. Sports field. Beach volleyball. Activity and entertainment programme. Tourist information. Mobile homes and chalets for rent. Off site: Martinsicuro (shops, cafés and restaurants). Abruzzo national park.

Open: 23 April - 19 September.

Directions: The site is located on the seafront at Martinsicuro. Leave the A14 autostrada at the Martinsicuro exit, to the south of San Benedetto del Tronto. Follow signs to the town centre and then to the site. GPS: 42.88118, 13.9207

Charges guide

Per unit incl. 2 persons and electricity	€ 15,00 - € 42,00

ITALY – Ugento

Camping Riva di Ugento

Litoranea Gallipoli, Santa Maria di Leuca, I-73059 Ugento (Puglia)
t: 083 393 3600 e: info@rivadiugento.it
alanrogers.com/IT68650 www.rivadiugento.it

Accommodation: ☑ Pitch ☑ Mobile home/chalet ☐ Hotel/B&B ☐ Apartment

There are some campsites where you can be comfortable, have all the amenities at hand and still feel you are connecting with nature. Under the pine and eucalyptus trees of the Bay of Taranto foreshore is Camping Riva di Ugento. Its 900 pitches are nestled in and around the sand dunes and the foreshore area. They have space and trees around them and the sizes differ as the environment dictates the shape of most. The sea is only a short walk from most pitches and some are at the water's edge. The site buildings resemble huge wooden umbrellas and are in sympathy with the environment. There are swimming and paddling pools, although these are expensive to use in high season. A free cinema also shows special events via satellite TV near the main bar and restaurant area. The area is sandy but well shaded, and the pine-scented sea breezes give the site a cool, fresh feel. This site has an isolated, natural ambiance that defies its size. We were sorry to leave the site which was by far the best we found in the area.

Special offers

Special offers on www.rivadiugento.it

You might like to know

The white sandy beach stretches for miles along the idyllic Salento peninsula. It slopes gently into the crystal-clear sea making it ideal for families with children, and for a romantic stroll at sunset.

- ☑ **Beach on site**
- ☐ **Beach within 1 km**
- ☑ **Sandy beach**
- ☐ **Blue Flag quality**
- ☑ **Lifeguard** *(high season)*
- ☑ **Sun lounger and/or deckchair hire**
- ☑ **Watersports** *(e.g. sailing or windsurfing)*
- ☑ **Snacks and drinks**
- ☑ **Sunshades/sunbeds**
- ☐ **Dogs allowed** *(on the beach)*

Facilities: Twenty toilet blocks all with WCs, showers and washbasins. New bathrooms. Bar. Restaurant and takeaway. Swimming and paddling pools. Tennis. Bicycle hire. Watersports incl. windsurfing school. Cinema. TV in bar. WiFi. Entertainment for children. Dogs are not accepted. A new play area for children has been added. Beach volleyball. Off site: Fishing. Riding 500 m. Boat launching 4 km. Golf 40 km.

Open: 15 May - 30 September.

Directions: From Bari take the Brindisi road to Lecce, then SS101 to Gallipoli, followed by the SR274 towards Sta Maria di Leuca, drive until exit called Felline and continue in direction of Torre San Giovanni, following the indications for Riva di Ugento. Site well signed and turn right at traffic lights on SS19. Bumpy approach road. GPS: 39.87475, 18.141117

Charges guide

Per unit incl. 2 persons, 1 child and electricity	€ 21,00 - € 45,00
extra person (over 2 yrs)	€ 5,00 - € 12,00

ITALY – Gallipoli

Camping Baia di Gallipoli

Litoranea per Santa Maria di Leuca, I-73014 Gallipoli (Puglia)
t: 083 327 3210 e: info@baiadigallipoli.com
alanrogers.com/IT68660 www.baiadigallipoli.com

Accommodation: ☑ Pitch ☑ Mobile home/chalet ☐ Hotel/B&B ☐ Apartment

The western shoreline of Puglia offers beaches of excellent quality, interspersed with small villages and some holiday complexes. The Baia di Gallipoli campsite is in a quiet rural area to the southwest of the town on a minor coast road. It offers 600 pitches, all with electricity, under pine and eucalyptus trees. Cars are parked in a separate area and access for vehicles is strictly controlled which gives the site a quiet, peaceful ambience. Although it is about 1 km. from the beach it has solved that problem in partnership with others by providing regular shuttle buses to the beach car park. The sites jointly fund a bar and restaurant on the beach with toilets and showers. The short walk to the beach from the car park is along a timber walkway and site staff clear the beach and the pine wood behind of rubbish daily. Michele Annese and the other staff clearly have a pride in their work and this is reflected in the standards offered and maintained. This is a good, quiet site in low season and also great for family holidays in July and August.

You might like to know

Why not hire a pedalo and explore some of the pretty coves accessible only from the sea?

- ☐ Beach on site
- ☑ Beach within 1 km
- ☑ Sandy beach
- ☐ Blue Flag quality
- ☐ Lifeguard *(high season)*
- ☑ Sun lounger and/or deckchair hire
- ☐ Watersports *(e.g. sailing or windsurfing)*
- ☑ Snacks and drinks
- ☑ Sunshades/sunbeds
- ☑ Dogs allowed *(on the beach)*

Facilities: Five toilet blocks include facilities for disabled visitors, both on the site and at the beach. Motorcaravan service point. Washing machines. Shop. Bar and restaurant (1/4-31/10). Swimming pool (1/6-30/9). Tennis. Shuttle bus to beach (1 km). Off site: Gallipoli.

Open: 1 April - 30 September.

Directions: The SS101 motorway south of Bari heads first to Lecce, then turns southwest towards Gallipoli. Join the SS274 towards Santa Maria di Leuca and exit at Lido Pizzo. Follow the coast road (SP215) towards Gallipoli and site is on the right 4 km. before Gallipoli.
GPS: 39.998317, 18.0265

Charges guide

Per unit incl. 2 persons and electricity	€ 23,50 - € 48,00
extra person	€ 8,50 - € 13,50
child (3-8 yrs)	free - € 8,00
dog	€ 1,50 - € 3,00

ITALY – Aglientu

Camping Baia Blu La Tortuga

Pineta di Vignola Mare, I-07020 Aglientu (Sardinia)
t: **079 602 200** e: **info@baiablu.com**
alanrogers.com/IT69550 www.baiaholiday.com

Accommodation: ☑ Pitch ☑ Mobile home/chalet ☐ Hotel/B&B ☐ Apartment

In the northeast of Sardinia and well situated for the Corsica ferry, Baia Blu is a large, professionally run campsite. The beach, with its golden sand, brilliant blue sea and pretty rocky outcrops, is warm and inviting. The site's 304 touring pitches (all with electricity), and almost as many mobile homes (most with air conditioning), are of fine sand and shaded by tall pines with banks of colourful oleanders and wide boulevards providing good access for units. Four exceptionally good toilet blocks provide a good ratio of excellent facilities to pitches, including some combined private shower and washbasin cabins for rent. This is a busy, bustling site with lots to do and attractive restaurants. There is a new bar/restaurant area with gazebos, a more casual beachside restaurant and bar, plus a self-service restaurant. The site is very popular with Italian families who enjoy the wide range of amenities here. It is used by many tour operators.

You might like to know

To the left of the bay is a beach of white sand. At the other end, there are rocks providing the perfect spot for those who love fishing.

- ☑ **Beach on site**
- ☐ **Beach within 1 km**
- ☑ **Sandy beach**
- ☐ **Blue Flag quality**
- ☐ **Lifeguard** *(high season)*
- ☑ **Sun lounger and/or deckchair hire**
- ☑ **Watersports** *(e.g. sailing or windsurfing)*
- ☑ **Snacks and drinks**
- ☑ **Sunshades/sunbeds**
- ☐ **Dogs allowed** *(on the beach)*

Facilities: Four excellent blocks (two with solar panels for hot water) with free hot showers, WCs, bidets and washbasins. Facilities for disabled campers. Washing machines and dryers. Motorcaravan services. Supermarket, new bar and restaurant, beachside restaurant and bar, self-service restaurant, snack bar and takeaway (all open 1/4-23/10). Gas. Bazaar. Gym. Hairdresser. Doctor's surgery. Playground. Tennis. Games and TV rooms. Windsurfing and diving schools. Internet point and WiFi area. Massage centre (July/Aug). Entertainment and sports activities (mid May-Sept). Excursions. Barbecue area (not permitted on pitches). Off site: Disco 50 m. Riding 18 km.

Open: 1 April - 22 October.

Directions: Site is on the north coast between towns of Costa Paradiso and S. Teresa di Gallura (18 km) at Pineta di Vignola Mare and is well signed. GPS: 41.07.463, 009.04.005

Charges guide

Per unit incl. 2 persons, water and electricity	€ 19,00 - € 51,00
tent pitch incl. electricity	€ 16,00 - € 41,00
extra person	€ 5,40 - € 13,40
child (3-9 yrs)	€ 3,40 - € 10,90
dog	€ 3,50 - € 7,50

GREECE – Neos Marmaras

Camping Areti

GR-63081 Neos Marmaras (Central Macedonia)
t: 237 507 1430 e: info@camping-areti.gr
alanrogers.com/GR8145 www.camping-areti.gr

Accommodation: ☑ Pitch ☑ Mobile home/chalet ☐ Hotel/B&B ☐ Apartment

If you imagine a typical Greek campsite as being set immediately behind a small sandy beach in a quiet cove with pitches amongst pine and olive trees, which stretch a long way back to the small coast road, then you have found your ideal site. Camping Areti is beautifully located just off the beaten track on the peninsula of Sithonia. Olive groves at the rear provide parking spaces for caravans and boats, and small boats can be launched from the beach. It has 130 pitches for touring units. The Charalambidi family maintain their site to very high standards and this is a site where visitors will not be disappointed. Olive, pine and eucalyptus trees provide shade for the grassed pitches and when we visited in mid June, there was a wonderful display of cacti in full bloom near the entrance. The site, with its quiet, picturesque location, good facilities and friendly management has justly won many recommendations and represents camping at its best; it is the ideal place to spend some time after the long journey to Greece.

You might like to know

The Spalathronisia, three small islands ideal for excursions and fishing, are just 300 m. from the beach.

- ☐ Beach on site
- ☑ Beach within 1 km
- ☑ Sandy beach
- ☐ Blue Flag quality
- ☐ Lifeguard *(high season)*
- ☐ Sun lounger and/or deckchair hire
- ☑ Watersports *(e.g. sailing or windsurfing)*
- ☑ Snacks and drinks
- ☐ Sunshades/sunbeds
- ☐ Dogs allowed *(on the beach)*

Facilities: Three excellent toilet blocks include showers, WCs and washbasins. Kitchen with sinks, electric hobs and fridges. Laundry with washing machines. Chemical disposal. Small shop and restaurant. Sandy beach. Bungalows to rent. Fishing, sailing and swimming. Communal barbecues. Off site: Riding, golf and bicycle hire 10 km. Sithonia, Mount Athos and the nearby Spalathronisia islands.

Open: 1 May - 31 October.

Directions: Although the postal address is Neos Marmaras the site is 12 km. south. So stay on the main coast road, past the casino resort at Porto Carras and 5 km. further on turn right towards the site (signed). Then turn right again down to the coast and turn left and on for 1.5 km. Turn right into site access road. Reception is 700 m. GPS: 40.024183, 23.81595

Charges guide

Per unit incl. 2 persons and electricity	€ 33,70 - € 37,00

No credit cards.

GREECE – Nafplio

Camping New Triton

Plaka Drepano, GR-21060 Nafplio (Peloponnese)
t: **275 209 2128**
alanrogers.com/GR8635

Accommodation: ☑ Pitch ☐ Mobile home/chalet ☐ Hotel/B&B ☐ Apartment

What do we look for in a good campsite in Greece? Given the excellent Greek weather, the answer is probably a good, flat pitch with some shade, excellent toilets and showers that are spotlessly clean, a small shop and proximity to a beach and local tavernas. Well, here you have it all! Under the control of the owners, Mr and Mrs George Christopoulous, this is an exceptional site with 40 good size touring pitches under high screens, just across the road from Drepano beach. Local tavernas are within strolling distance and the town's shops are 1.2 km. away. Personal management and supervision clearly works and this small site sets very high standards that others often fail to achieve.

You might like to know

Close to the Drepano beach are small pool areas where blue and white cranes live and breed. Deprano village is 1.2 km. away with a choice of tavernas and local bars.

- ☐ **Beach on site**
- ☑ **Beach within 1 km**
- ☑ **Sandy beach**
- ☐ **Blue Flag quality**
- ☐ **Lifeguard** *(high season)*
- ☐ **Sun lounger and/or deckchair hire**
- ☑ **Watersports** *(e.g. sailing or windsurfing)*
- ☑ **Snacks and drinks**
- ☐ **Sunshades/sunbeds**
- ☑ **Dogs allowed** *(on the beach)*

Facilities: Excellent refurbished toilet blocks include showers, WCs and washbasins. Baby bath. Facilities for disabled visitors. Chemical disposal. Laundry with washing machines and ironing board. Electric hobs for cooking. Fridge and freezer. Small shop (1/6-30/9).
Off site: Drepano beach, local tavernas and bars.

Open: 1 April - 30 October.

Directions: From Nafplio follow the main road west and then turn right towards Drepano. In the town follow the signs Plaka Drepano and turn left towards the coast. At the beach turn right and site is just ahead. GPS: 37.53202, 22.89165

Charges guide

Per unit incl. 2 persons and electricity	€ 23,00

GREECE – Finikounda

Camping Finikes

GR-24006 Finikounda (Peloponnese)
t: 272 302 8524 e: camping-finikes@otenet.gr
alanrogers.com/GR8695 www.finikescamping.gr

Accommodation: ☑ Pitch ☑ Mobile home/chalet ☐ Hotel/B&B ☐ Apartment

This site offers 80 level pitches with good shade and great views, and 16 apartments to rent. Some pitches have high reed screens that give good protection from the blazing Greek sun and the turquoise sea is great for swimming, windsurfing and sailing. The site is at the western corner of Finikounda Bay and has direct access to the sandy beach by crossing small natural dunes. The facilities are excellent and in low season, when there are 18 or less campers, each camper is given the keys to a WC and shower for their own personal use. The small picturesque village, three kilometres to the east, is at the back of the bay. Caiques and fishing boats are drawn up all along the sandy shore here, while tavernas serve their fresh catch along the water's edge.

You might like to know

An attractive path runs across the dunes from the site to the beach, which is excellent for children. The town of Finikounda is a twenty minute walk along the beach.

- ☑ Beach on site
- ☐ Beach within 1 km
- ☑ Sandy beach
- ☐ Blue Flag quality
- ☐ Lifeguard *(high season)*
- ☐ Sun lounger and/or deckchair hire
- ☑ Watersports *(e.g. sailing or windsurfing)*
- ☐ Snacks and drinks
- ☐ Sunshades/sunbeds
- ☐ Dogs allowed *(on the beach)*

Facilities: The good toilet block includes showers, WCs and washbasins. Facilities for disabled visitors. Kitchen includes sinks, electric hobs and fridges. Laundry. Chemical disposal. Bar, small shop and restaurant. Accommodation to rent. Off site: Finikounda and the Inouse Islands. Distance to boat launching and sailing 3 km. Bicycle hire 25 km.

Open: All year.

Directions: Site is 3 km. from the centre of Finikounda. From the village head west and turn left into the site. GPS: 36.802817, 21.78105

Charges guide

Per unit incl. 2 persons and electricity	€ 21,00 - € 24,00

No credit cards.

GREECE – Pylos

Camping Navarino Beach

Gialova, GR-24001 Pylos (Peloponnese)
t: **272 302 2973** e: **info@navarino-beach.gr**
alanrogers.com/GR8705 www.navarino-beach.gr

Accommodation: ☑ Pitch ☑ Mobile home/chalet ☐ Hotel/B&B ☐ Apartment

Situated directly on the beach in the historic Bay of Navarino, there can be very few sites in this guide that have the wonderful position this one occupies. It is superb and has the most amazing sunset to complement that. There are 150 pitches, most facing the beach, with 30 being directly situated alongside. All have electricity (10A) and most have good shade. The pitches are arranged in rows to ensure that all have beach access. The facilities are adequate and cleaned regularly. The staff are friendly and efficient, and there is a very good restaurant with a terrace directly by the beach. The light wind in the morning which strengthens on some afternoons makes it a great windsurfing location and boats can be moored by the beach. The site is split into two, with the section across the road used mainly for tents or as the overspill. There is plenty of shade. The beach is sandy and shelves gently making it incredibly safe for children. This site is highly recommended.

You might like to know

The shallow blue water on this sandy beach is safe for children. The campsite recommend a visit to the Divary Lagoon, considered to be one of the most important lagoons in Greece.

- ☑ **Beach on site**
- ☐ **Beach within 1 km**
- ☑ **Sandy beach**
- ☐ **Blue Flag quality**
- ☐ **Lifeguard** *(high season)*
- ☐ **Sun lounger and/or deckchair hire**
- ☑ **Watersports** *(e.g. sailing or windsurfing)*
- ☐ **Snacks and drinks**
- ☑ **Sunshades/sunbeds**
- ☑ **Dogs allowed** *(on the beach)*

Facilities: The five toilet blocks are well situated and, even in high season, were kept very clean and never became overcrowded. There are open washbasins, hot water to showers, and communal refrigerators and freezers. There is a small shop where basic provisions can be purchased. Other shops within walking distance. Dogs are accepted but must be kept on a lead and out of the sea. Off site: Within walking distance of Gialova with its promenade restaurants. Pylos 6 km. Nestors Palace 12 km. Numerous places to visit.

Open: All year, full facilities Easter - October.

Directions: Directly on the National Road Pylos Kyparissia. 300 metres from the village of Gialova. GPS: 36.94764, 21.70618

Charges guide

Per unit incl. 2 persons and electricity	€ 23,00 - € 25,00
extra person	€ 6,00
child	€ 3,00

HUNGARY – Révfülöp

Balatontourist Camping Napfény

Halász u. 5, H-8253 Révfülöp (Veszprem County)
t: 87 563 031 e: napfeny@balatontourist.hu
alanrogers.com/HU5370 www.balatontourist.hu

Accommodation: ☑ Pitch ☑ Mobile home/chalet ☐ Hotel/B&B ☐ Apartment

Camping Napfény, an exceptionally good site, is designed for families with children of all ages looking for an active holiday, and has a 200 m. frontage on Lake Balaton. The site's 370 pitches vary in size (60-110 sq.m) and almost all have shade – very welcome during the hot Hungarian summers – and 6-10A electricity. As with most of the sites on Lake Balaton, a train line runs just outside the site boundary. There are steps to get into the lake and canoes, boats and pedaloes for hire. An extensive entertainment programme is designed for all ages and there are several bars and restaurants of various styles. There are souvenir shops and a supermarket. In fact, you need not leave the site at all during your holiday, although there are several excursions on offer, including to Budapest and to some of the many Hungarian spas, trips over Lake Balaton and traditional wine tour.

You might like to know

There are grassy beaches at the lakeside, where pedaloes and boats are for hire. Fishing is also popular on the lake.

- ☑ **Beach on site**
- ☐ **Beach within 1 km**
- ☐ **Sandy beach**
- ☐ **Blue Flag quality**
- ☐ **Lifeguard** *(high season)*
- ☐ **Sun lounger and/or deckchair hire**
- ☑ **Watersports** *(e.g. sailing or windsurfing)*
- ☐ **Snacks and drinks**
- ☐ **Sunshades/sunbeds**
- ☐ **Dogs allowed** *(on the beach)*

Facilities: The three excellent sanitary blocks have toilets, washbasins (open style and in cabins) with hot and cold water, spacious showers (both preset and controllable), child size toilets and basins, and two bathrooms (hourly charge). Heated baby room. Facilities for disabled campers. Launderette. Dog shower. Motorcaravan services. Supermarket. Bars, restaurants and souvenir shop. Children's pool. Sports field. Minigolf. Fishing. Bicycle hire. Canoe, rowing boats and pedalo hire. Varied entertainment programme for all ages. Internet (charged). Off site: Tennis 300 m. Riding 3 km.

Open: 30 April - 30 September.

Directions: Follow road 71 from Veszprém southeast to Keszthely. Site is in Révfülöp. GPS: 46.829469, 17.640164

Charges guide

Per unit incl. 2 persons and electricity	HUF 3400 - 7150
extra person	HUF 800 - 1200
child (2-14 yrs)	HUF 550 - 900
dog	HUF 550 - 900

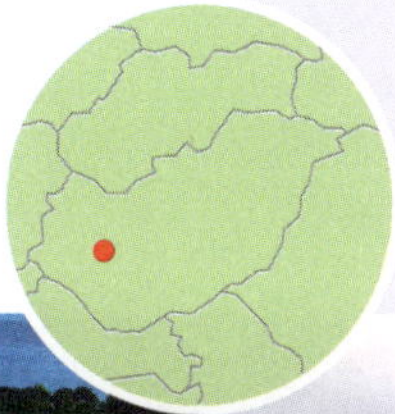

SWITZERLAND – Tenero

Camping Campofelice

Via alle Brere 7, CH-6598 Tenero (Ticino)
t: **091 745 1417** e: **camping@campofelice.ch**
alanrogers.com/CH9890 www.campofelice.ch

Accommodation: ☑ Pitch ☑ Mobile home/chalet ☐ Hotel/B&B ☐ Apartment

The largest site in Switzerland, it is bordered on the front by Lake Maggiore and on one side by the Verzasca estuary, where the site has its own marina. Campofelice is divided into rows, with 860 generously sized, individual pitches on flat grass on either side of hard access roads. Mostly well shaded, all pitches have electricity connections (10/13A) and 409 also have water, drainage and TV connections. Pitches near the lake cost more (these are not available for motorcaravans until September) and a special area is reserved for small tents. The sheer quality of this superb site justifies the higher than average prices. Sporting facilities are good and there are cycle paths in the area, including into Locarno. The beach by the lake is sandy, long and wider than the usual lakeside ones. It shelves gently so that bathing is safe for children. Within a demarcated area are floating trampolines and rafts, and a specially marked section for toddlers.

You might like to know

The site is set on the sandy shores of Lake Maggiore, where there is safe swimming and a private beach. Kayaks and canoes are available to hire from the site's own harbour.

☑ **Beach on site**
☐ **Beach within 1 km**
☑ **Sandy beach**
☐ **Blue Flag quality**
☑ **Lifeguard** *(high season)*
☐ **Sun lounger and/or deckchair hire**
☐ **Watersports** *(e.g. sailing or windsurfing)*
☑ **Snacks and drinks**
☐ **Sunshades/sunbeds**
☐ **Dogs allowed** *(on the beach)*

Facilities: The six toilet blocks (three heated) are of exemplary quality. Washing machines and dryers. Motorcaravan services. Gas supplies. Supermarket, restaurant, bar and takeaway (all season). Snack kiosk at beach. Lifeguards on duty. Tennis. Minigolf. Bicycle hire. Canoe and pedalo hire. Boat launching. Playgrounds. Doctor calls. Dogs are not accepted. New chalet for disabled visitors. Camping accessories shop. Car hire. Car wash. WiFi (charged). Off site: Fishing 500 m. Water skiing and windsurfing 1 km. Riding 5 km. Golf 8 km. Boatyard with maintenance facilities.

Open: 22 March - 31 October.

Directions: On the Bellinzona - Locarno road 13, exit Tenero. Site is signed at roundabout. Coming from the south, enter Tenero and follow signs to site. GPS: 46.168611, 8.855556

Charges guide

Per unit incl. 2 persons and electricity	CHF 38,00 - 82,00
extra person	CHF 8,00 - 11,00

CROATIA – Porec

Camping Lanterna

Lanterna 1, HR-52465 Porec (Istria)
t: 052 465 010 e: camping@valamar.com
alanrogers.com/CR6716 www.camping-adriatic.com

Accommodation: ☑ Pitch ☑ Mobile home/chalet ☐ Hotel/B&B ☐ Apartment

This is a well organised site and one of the largest in Croatia with high standards and an amazing selection of activities, and is part of the Camping on the Adriatic group. Set in 80 hectares with over 3 kilometres of beach, there are 2,851 pitches, of which 1,887 are for touring units. All have electricity (10A) and fresh water and 225 also have waste water drainage. Pitches are 80-120 sq.m. with some superb locations right on the sea, although these tend to be taken first so it is advisable to book ahead. Some of the better pitches are in a 'reserved booking' area. There are wonderful coastal views from some of the well shaded terraced pitches. Facilities at Lanterna are impressive with the whole operation running smoothly for the campers. The land is sloping in parts and terraced in others. There is a pool complex including a large pool for children, in addition to the pretty bay with its rocky beaches and buoyed safety areas. Many activities and quality entertainment for all are available both on and off site.

You might like to know

Transport between the campsite and airports can be arranged for passengers arriving at Trieste, Treviso, Pula and Krk.

- ☑ **Beach on site**
- ☐ **Beach within 1 km**
- ☐ **Sandy beach**
- ☑ **Blue Flag quality**
- ☑ **Lifeguard** *(high season)*
- ☑ **Sun lounger and/or deckchair hire**
- ☑ **Watersports** *(e.g. sailing or windsurfing)*
- ☑ **Snacks and drinks**
- ☑ **Sunshades/sunbeds**
- ☑ **Dogs allowed** *(on the beach)*

Facilities: The sixteen sanitary blocks are clean and good quality. Baby changing. Some Turkish style WCs, hot showers. Facilities for disabled visitors in some blocks. Three supermarkets. Fresh fish shop. Four restaurants, bars and snack bars and fast food outlets. Swimming pool and two paddling pools. Sandpit and play areas. Entertainment in high season. Tennis. Bicycle hire. Watersports. Boat hire. Minigolf. Riding. Internet café. Jetty for boats. WiFi (free). Pets are accepted in certain areas. Off site: Hourly bus service. Fishing. Riding 500 m. Golf 2 km. Nearest large supermarket in Novigrad 9 km.

Open: 1 April - 10 October.

Directions: The turn to Lanterna is well signed off the Novigrad to Porec road about 8 km. south of Novigrad. Continue for about 2 km. down turn off road towards coast and the site is on the right hand side. GPS: 45.29672, 13.59442

Charges guide

Per unit incl. 2 persons and electricity	€ 16,90 - € 31,00
with full services	€ 18,30 - € 32,60
extra person	€ 4,40 - € 7,90
child (4-10 yrs)	free - € 5,40

Prices for pitches by the sea are higher.

CROATIA – Porec

Naturist Resort Solaris

Lanterna bb, HR-52440 Porec (Istria)
t: **052 465 110** e: **camping-porec@valamar.com**
alanrogers.com/CR6718 www.camping-adriatic.com

Accommodation: ☑ Pitch ☑ Mobile home/chalet ☑ Hotel/B&B ☑ Apartment

This naturist site is part of the Camping on the Adriatic group and has a most pleasant atmosphere. When we visited in high season there were lots of happy people having fun. A pretty cove and lots of beach frontage with cool pitches under trees makes the site very attractive. Of the 1,333 pitches, 550 are available for touring, with 600 long stay units. There are 145 fully serviced pitches (100 sq.m) available on a 'first come, first served' basis, with an ample supply of electricity hook-ups (10/16A) and plentiful water points. As this is a naturist site, please follow the rules. There is a small, but very pleasant swimming pool close to the sea which has a lifeguard (clothing is not allowed in the pool). Apartments and rooms with half board are available to rent. For those who embrace the naturist regime or want to give it a try, this is a pleasant, quiet site with above average facilities in an area of outstanding natural beauty.

Special offers

There is a choice of apartment accommodation, and transport can be organised between the airport and the site.

You might like to know

Please note: this is a naturist campsite. Pets are permitted in certain areas of the campsite. There is the Maro mini club, beach volleyball pitch, children's sandpit and entertainment programmes.

- ☑ **Beach on site**
- ☐ **Beach within 1 km**
- ☐ **Sandy beach**
- ☑ **Blue Flag quality**
- ☑ **Lifeguard** *(high season)*
- ☐ **Sun lounger and/or deckchair hire**
- ☑ **Watersports** *(e.g. sailing or windsurfing)*
- ☑ **Snacks and drinks**
- ☐ **Sunshades/sunbeds**
- ☐ **Dogs allowed** *(on the beach)*

Facilities: Eleven excellent, fully equipped toilet blocks provide toilets, washbasins and showers. Some blocks have facilities for disabled visitors. Washing machines and ironing. Restaurants, grills and fast food, and supermarkets. Swimming pool. Tennis. Bicycle hire. Riding. Play areas. Boat launching. Car wash. Entertainment. WiFi (free). Dogs are restricted to a particular area and are not allowed on the beach. Off site: Riding and fishing 500 m. Excursions.

Open: 1 April - 10 October.

Directions: Site is 8 km. south of Novigrad on the Novigrad - Porec road. Turn towards the coast signed Lanterna. Continue straight on down this road and after passing the security barrier, turn left to Solaris.
GPS: 45.29126, 13.5848

Charges guide

Per unit incl. 2 persons and electricity	€ 15,60 - € 27,90
with full services	€ 17,50 - € 30,20
extra person	€ 4,10 - € 7,10
child (4-10 yrs)	free - € 5,00

CROATIA – Rovinj

Naturist Camping Valalta

Cesta Valalta-Lim bb, HR-52210 Rovinj (Istria)
t: **052 804 800** e: **valalta@valalta.hr**
alanrogers.com/CR6731 www.valalta.hr

Accommodation: ☑ Pitch ☑ Mobile home/chalet ☐ Hotel/B&B ☐ Apartment

This is a most impressive site for up to 6,000 naturist campers, which has a pleasant, open feel. The passage through reception is efficient and this feeling is maintained around the well organised site. A friendly, family atmosphere is to be found here. Valalta is a family oriented campsite. All pitches are the same price with 16A electricity, although they vary in size and surroundings. The variations include shade, views, sand, grass, sea frontage, level ground, slopes and terracing. It is not possible to reserve a particular pitch and campers do move pitches at will. The impressive pool is in lagoon style with water features and cascades. Unusually for Croatia, the beach has soft sand (with some help from imported sand). All manner of sports are available and a marina forms part of the site. The high standard here and throughout the campsite has ensured that customers have returned regularly since its opening in 1968. We were impressed by this well ordered and smart naturist site.

You might like to know

This naturist campsite has seawater swimming pools, numerous shingle bays and over 5 km. of beaches. Visitors can enjoy a refreshing beer from the site's own brewery!

- ☑ **Beach on site**
- ☐ **Beach within 1 km**
- ☑ **Sandy beach**
- ☐ **Blue Flag quality**
- ☑ **Lifeguard** *(high season)*
- ☑ **Sun lounger and/or deckchair hire**
- ☐ **Watersports** *(e.g. sailing or windsurfing)*
- ☑ **Snacks and drinks**
- ☑ **Sunshades/sunbeds**
- ☐ **Dogs allowed** *(on the beach)*

Facilities: Twenty high quality new or refurbished sanitary blocks of which four are smaller units of plastic 'pod' construction. Hot showers (coin operated). Facilities for disabled campers. Washing machines and dryers. Supermarket. Four restaurants (one specialising in seafood). Pizzeria. Two bars. Large lagoon style pool complex. Beauty salon. Fitness club. Massage. Minigolf. Tennis. Sailing. Play area. Bicycle hire. Beach (volleyball). Marina with full services. Internet. Entertainment all season. Kindergarten. Dogs are not accepted. Off site: Riding 7 km.

Open: 25 April - 26 September.

Directions: Site is on the coast 8 km. north of Rovinj. If approaching from north turn inland (follow signs to Rovinj) to drive around the Limski Kanal. Follow signs towards Valalta about 2 km. east of Rovinj. Site is at the end of the road and is well signed. GPS: 45.12235, 13.632083

Charges guide

Per unit incl. 2 persons and electricity	€ 26,80 - € 44,80
extra person	€ 8,80 - € 16,30
child (4-14 yrs)	€ 2,50 - € 5,50

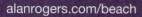

CROATIA – Rovinj

Camping Polari

Polari bb, HR-52210 Rovinj (Istria)
t: **052 801 501** e: **polari@maistra.hr**
alanrogers.com/CR6732 www.CampingRovinjVrsar.com

Accommodation: ☑ Pitch ☑ Mobile home/chalet ☐ Hotel/B&B ☐ Apartment

This 60-hectare site has excellent facilities for both textile and naturist campers, the latter in an area of 12 hectares to the left of the main site. There is shade here from a good covering of trees. In all, the site has 1,650 pitches for touring units which are level with some shade. All have access to 10A electricity. There is something to enjoy for everyone here or you may prefer just to relax in this quiet location. An impressive swimming pool complex is child friendly with large paddling areas. The ancient town of Rovinj is well worth a visit, although parking is difficult. It is best reached via the 4.5 km. coastal cycle path or by bus from the campsite. Part of the Maistra Group, a massive improvement programme has been undertaken and the result makes it a very attractive option. Enjoy a meal on the huge restaurant terrace with panoramic views of the sea.

You might like to know

Camping Polari is located in a picturesque cove with over 2 km. of attractive coastline and plentiful shade from the summer sun. There is a new swimming pool and extensive sports provision.

☑ **Beach on site**
☐ **Beach within 1 km**
☐ **Sandy beach**
☑ **Blue Flag quality**
☑ **Lifeguard** *(high season)*
☑ **Sun lounger and/or deckchair hire**
☑ **Watersports** *(e.g. sailing or windsurfing)*
☑ **Snacks and drinks**
☑ **Sunshades/sunbeds**
☑ **Dogs allowed** *(on the beach)*

Facilities: All the sanitary facilities have been renovated to a high standard with plenty of hot water and good showers. Washing machines and dryers. Laundry service including ironing. Motorcaravan service point. Two shops, one large and one small, one restaurant and snack bar. Tennis. Minigolf. Children's entertainment with all major European languages spoken. Bicycle hire. Watersports. Sailing school.
Off site: Riding 1 km. Five buses daily to and from Rovinj 3 km. Golf 30 km.

Open: 1 April - 2 October.

Directions: From any access road to Rovinj look for red signs to AC Polari (amongst other destinations). The site is about 3 km. south of Rovinj. GPS: 45.06286, 13.67489

Charges guide

Per unit incl. 2 persons and electricity	€ 18,00 - € 36,10
extra person (18-64 yrs)	€ 5,00 - € 9,30
child (5-17 yrs)	€ 4,00 - € 7,50
dog	€ 3,10 - € 6,50

CROATIA – Cres

Camping Kovacine

Melin I/20, HR-51557 Cres (Kvarner)
t: 051 573 150 e: campkovacine@kovacine.com
alanrogers.com/CR6765 www.camp-kovacine.com

Accommodation: ☑ Pitch ☑ Mobile home/chalet ☐ Hotel/B&B ☐ Apartment

Camping Kovacine is located on a peninsula on the beautiful Kvarner island of Cres, just 2 km. from the town of the same name. The site has 750 numbered, mostly level pitches, of which 632 are for tourers (300 with 12A electricity). On sloping ground, partially shaded by mature olive and pine trees, pitching is on the large, open spaces between the trees. Some places have views of the Valun lagoon. Kovacine is partly an FKK (naturist) site, which is quite common in Croatia, and has a pleasant atmosphere. Here one can enjoy local live music on a stage close to the pebble beach (Blue Flag), where there is also a restaurant and bar. The site has its own beach, part concrete, part pebbles, and a jetty for mooring boats and fishing. It is close to the historic town of Cres, the main town on the island, which offers a rich history of fishing, shipyards and authentic Kvarner-style houses. There are also several bars, restaurants and shops.

Special offers

Ferry costs refunded for 10- and 18-night stays. 7 nights for 6 and 14 for 12 in low season. Free WiFi.

You might like to know

Kovacine has 750 pitches and a number of mobile homes for rent. Special facilities enable disabled visitors to access the sea. Airport transfer service between Rijeka-Cres and site.

☑ Beach on site
☐ Beach within 1 km
☐ Sandy beach
☑ Blue Flag quality
☑ Lifeguard *(high season)*
☐ Sun lounger and/or deckchair hire
☑ Watersports *(e.g. sailing or windsurfing)*
☑ Snacks and drinks
☐ Sunshades/sunbeds
☑ Dogs allowed *(on the beach)*

Facilities: Modern, comfortable toilet blocks (two refurbished) offer British style toilets, equipped with solar power, open plan washbasins (some cabins for ladies) and hot showers. Private family bathroom for hire. Facilities for disabled visitors plus facilities for children. Laundry sinks and washing machine. Fridge box hire. Motorcaravan service point. Car wash. Mini-marina and boat crane. Supermarket. Bar, restaurant and pizzeria. New swimming pool. Playground. Daily children's club. Evening shows with live music. Boat launching. Fishing. Diving centre. Motorboat hire. Free WiFi. Airport transfers. Off site: Wellness and fitness centre 0.5 km. Historic town of Cres with bars, restaurants and shops 2 km.

Open: 16 April - 15 October.

Directions: From Rijeka take no. 2 road south towards Labin and take ferry to Cres at Brestova. Continue to Cres and follow site signs.
GPS: 44.96188, 14.39650

Charges guide

Per unit incl. 2 persons and electricity	€ 16,30 - € 31,80
extra person	€ 5,50 - € 10,80
child (3-12 yrs)	€ 2,60 - € 4,40
dog	€ 1,00 - € 3,00

FRANCE – Saint Georges-d'Oléron

Camping les Gros Joncs

850 route de Ponthezieres, F-17190 Saint Georges-d'Oléron (Charente-Maritime)
t: **05 46 76 52 29** e: **info@les-gros-joncs.fr**
alanrogers.com/FR17070 **www.les-gros-joncs.fr**

Accommodation: ☑ Pitch ☑ Mobile home/chalet ☐ Hotel/B&B ☐ Apartment

Situated on the west coast of the island of Ile d'Oléron, les Gros Joncs is owned and run by the Cavel family who work hard to keep the site up to date and of high quality. There are 50 or so touring pitches of a good size (some extra large) with tall pine trees providing a choice between full sun and varying degrees of shade. All have water and 12A electricity to hand. The main building houses a light and airy reception and also a beautifully presented modern bar and restaurant, a fully stocked and competitively priced shop, an attractive indoor swimming pool and a magnificent spa. The indoor pool, with water jets and jacuzzi, has glass sides, which in good weather are opened out onto an outdoor pool area where there are also water slides, a paddling area and plenty of sunbathing terraces. Both pools are heated. The spa offers hydrotherapy and beauty treatments, sauna, and a comprehensive fitness room. Much attention has been given to the needs of disabled visitors here, including chalets which are specially adapted.

You might like to know

Our heated open-air pools include a large swimming pool, an adventure paddling pool and a toboggan. The indoor pool also has a whirlpool, lazy river, anatomical seats and powerful water jets.

- ☑ **Beach on site**
- ☑ **Beach within 1 km**
- ☑ **Sandy beach**
- ☐ **Blue Flag quality**
- ☐ **Lifeguard** *(high season)*
- ☐ **Sun lounger and/or deckchair hire**
- ☐ **Watersports** *(e.g. sailing or windsurfing)*
- ☐ **Snacks and drinks**
- ☐ **Sunshades/sunbeds**
- ☐ **Dogs allowed** *(on the beach)*

Facilities: Traditional style toilet facilities are maintained to a high standard. Laundry facilities. Motorcaravan services. Well stocked shop with bakery and restaurant (all year). Indoor pool with first class spa and wellness centre (all year, with professional staff). Heated outdoor pool (1/4-15/9). Children's clubs (1/7-15/9). Bicycle hire. Internet access and WiFi (charged). ATM. No charcoal barbecues. Off site: Beach 200 or 400 m. via a sandy path. Bus service from Chéray. Fishing 2 km. Riding 6 km. Golf 8 km.

Open: All year.

Directions: Cross the viaduct onto the Ile d'Oléron. Take D734 (St Georges-d'Oléron). At traffic lights in Chéray turn left. Follow signs for camping and Sable Vignier. Soon signs indicate directions to Les Gros Joncs.
GPS: 45.95356, -1.37979

Charges guide

Per unit incl. 2 persons and electricity	€ 18,70 - € 46,10
extra person	€ 6,12 - € 12,00
child (0-7 yrs)	€ 2,80 - € 7,40
dog	€ 3,00

FRANCE – La Flotte-en-Ré

Camping les Peupliers

RD735, F-17630 La Flotte-en-Ré (Charente-Maritime)
t: 02 51 33 17 00 e: camping@les-peupliers.com
alanrogers.com/FR17290 www.camp-atlantique.com

Accommodation: ☑ Pitch ☑ Mobile home/chalet ☐ Hotel/B&B ☐ Apartment

On the Ile de Ré, you are never far from the sea and the location of this campsite is no exception. It is just 800 metres from the sea with sea views from some of the pitches. English is spoken at reception and the staff go out of their way to make your stay enjoyable. The 20 level touring pitches are in a separate area from 143 chalets for rent, in an area of light woodland. There are few water points. The trees provide some shade, but the very low hedges provide little privacy as the width and length of the pitches varies. The pitches are long enough for large units, including American motorhomes and twin axle caravans, although access to some pitches is difficult (prior booking necessary). The site is within walking distance of the shops and restaurants of the pretty fishing port of Flotte-en-Ré. With 100 km. of cycle tracks, sandy beaches, local markets and a uniquely sunny micro-climate, this a great place to sample island life. Historic La Rochelle on the mainland is one of France's most captivating ports.

You might like to know

A fine sandy beach is 800 m. from the site and is protected by dunes and pine trees. Nearby, in Flotte-en-Ré, there is a sailing school, catamaran sailing trips and sea fishing.

- ☐ **Beach on site**
- ☑ **Beach within 1 km**
- ☑ **Sandy beach**
- ☐ **Blue Flag quality**
- ☑ **Lifeguard** *(high season)*
- ☐ **Sun lounger and/or deckchair hire**
- ☑ **Watersports** *(e.g. sailing or windsurfing)*
- ☐ **Snacks and drinks**
- ☐ **Sunshades/sunbeds**
- ☐ **Dogs allowed** *(on the beach)*

Facilities: Two new but traditionally designed sanitary blocks are clean and well maintained. Both have unisex facilities including showers and vanity type units in cabins. Separate facilities for disabled visitors. Laundry facilities. Shop, restaurant, takeaway and bar with TV (all 2/4-24/9). Heated outdoor swimming pool (21/5-24/9). Play area. Children's club and entertainment (high season). Fridge hire. Bicycle hire. Max. 1 dog. WiFi throughout (charged). Off site: Riding 500 m. Beach, fishing, boat launching and sailing 800 m. Golf 20 km.

Open: 2 April - 24 September.

Directions: Over the toll bridge and turn left at second roundabout. Site is well signed. GPS: 46.18461, -1.3080

Charges guide

Per unit incl. 2 persons and electricity	€ 21,00 - € 35,00
extra person	€ 5,00 - € 9,00
child (under 5 yrs)	free - € 6,00
dog (max. 1)	€ 5,00

FRANCE – La Brée-les-Bains

Camping Antioche d'Oléron

Route de Proires, F-17840 La Brée-les-Bains (Charente-Maritime)
t: **05 46 47 92 00** e: **info@camping-antiochedoleron.com**
alanrogers.com/FR17570 www.camping-antiochedoleron.com

Accommodation: ☑ Pitch ☑ Mobile home/chalet ☐ Hotel/B&B ☐ Apartment

Situated to the northeast of the island, Camping Antioche is quietly located within a five minute walk of the beach. There are 130 pitches, of which 73 are occupied by mobile homes and 57 are for touring units. The pitches are set amongst attractive shrubs and palm trees and all have electricity (10A), water and a drain. A new pool area which comprises two swimming pools (heated), two jacuzzis, two paddling pools and a raised sunbathing deck, is beautifully landscaped with palms and flowers. A small bar, restaurant and takeaway offer reasonably priced food and drinks. The site becomes livelier in season with regular evening entertainment and activities for all the family. With specially prepared trails for cycling, and oyster farms and salt flats to visit, the Ile d'Oléron offers something for everyone. Bresnais market, selling local produce and products, is within easy access on foot and is held daily in high season.

You might like to know

One area of the beach is dedicated to watersports and pleasure boats. At low tide there is a flat rocky area perfect for fishing.

- ☐ **Beach on site**
- ☑ **Beach within 1 km**
- ☑ **Sandy beach**
- ☐ **Blue Flag quality**
- ☑ **Lifeguard** *(high season)*
- ☐ **Sun lounger and/or deckchair hire**
- ☑ **Watersports** *(e.g. sailing or windsurfing)*
- ☑ **Snacks and drinks**
- ☐ **Sunshades/sunbeds**
- ☐ **Dogs allowed** *(on the beach)*

Facilities: The single sanitary block is of a good standard and is kept clean and fresh. Facilities for disabled visitors. Laundry. Motorcaravan services. Bar, restaurant and snack bar (weekends only May and June, daily July/Aug). Swimming and paddling pools. Games room. Play area. WiFi. Bicycle hire (July/Aug). Off site: Beach and fishing 150 m. Riding 1.5 km. Golf 7 km.

Open: 1 April - 30 September.

Directions: Cross the bridge on the D26 and join the D734. After St Georges turn right onto the D273E1 towards La Brée-les-Baines. At T-junction turn left from where the campsite is signed. GPS: 46.02007, -1.35764

Charges guide

Per unit incl. 2 persons and electricity	€ 22,30 - € 37,30
extra person	€ 7,50 - € 8,70
child (1-14 yrs)	€ 4,20 - € 5,40
dog	€ 4,20

FRANCE – Boyardville

Camping Signol

121 avenue des Albatros, F-17190 Boyardville (Charente-Maritime)
t: **02 51 33 17 00** e: **contact@signol.com**
alanrogers.com/FR17600 www.camp-atlantique.com

Accommodation: ☑ Pitch ☑ Mobile home/chalet ☐ Hotel/B&B ☐ Apartment

Occupying an eight-hectare site, just 800 metres from the sandy beaches, this campsite has plenty to offer. Of the 300 pitches, 107 are for touring and are set amongst high pine trees and one metre high hedges give plenty of shade and privacy; some have sea views. The pitches are generous (80-120 sq.m) although access to some is tight and may not be suitable for larger units. Levelling blocks are required on some. Electricity (6A) is available to all, although long leads are required occasionally as hook-ups can be shared between three or four pitches. There may be a short walk to the water supply. The facilities for children are in a fenced area and include climbing frames, bouncy castle and multisport court. The heated and supervised swimming pools are overlooked by the bar/snack bar. A club for children is organised in high season and treasure hunts and other activities are organised daily. Entertainment for adults is also arranged in high season.

You might like to know

The beautiful fine-sand beaches of Boyardville are only 800 m. away, from where there is a wonderful view of Fort Boyard. Cycle tracks criss-cross the oyster canals and Saumonards Forest.

- ☐ **Beach on site**
- ☑ **Beach within 1 km**
- ☑ **Sandy beach**
- ☐ **Blue Flag quality**
- ☑ **Lifeguard** *(high season)*
- ☐ **Sun lounger and/or deckchair hire**
- ☐ **Watersports** *(e.g. sailing or windsurfing)*
- ☑ **Snacks and drinks**
- ☐ **Sunshades/sunbeds**
- ☐ **Dogs allowed** *(on the beach)*

Facilities: Three modern, fully equipped toilet blocks provide washbasins and showers in cubicles. Facilities for disabled campers, and for children. Laundry. Motorcaravan services. No shop. Bar/snack bar, terrace, takeaway, breakfast service. Two swimming pools (21/5-12/9). Enclosed play area. Children's club (from 1/7). Boules. Evening entertainment (from 1/7). WiFi (free). Dogs are not accepted in July/Aug. Communal barbecues only. Mobile homes and chalets to hire. Off site: Nearest beach 800 m. Sailing and windsurfing. Fishing. Riding. Cycle and walking trails. St Pierre-d'Oléron (with shops, restaurants and supermarket).

Open: 1 May - 12 September.

Directions: Cross the viaduct and continue on the D26 to Dolus and turn right on D126 signed Boyardville. Continue for 6 km. to canal bridge at edge of the town. Cross bridge and turn immediately sharp right along the quayside. Site signed from here. GPS: 45.96807, -1.24456

Charges guide

Per unit incl. 2 persons and electricity	€ 21,00 - € 35,00
extra person	€ 5,00 - € 9,00
child (under 5 yrs)	free - € 6,00

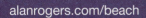

FRANCE – Saint Denis-d'Oléron

Les Hameaux des Marines

Rue des Seulières, F-17650 Saint Denis-d'Oléron (Charente-Maritime)
t: **05 55 84 34 48** e: **info@chalets-en-france.com**
alanrogers.com/FR17660 www.chalets-en-france.com

Accommodation: ☐ Pitch ☑ Mobile home/chalet ☐ Hotel/B&B ☐ Apartment

Les Hameaux des Marines is a member of the Chalets en France group. This group comprises four chalet parks in southern France. Please note, however, that there are no touring pitches here. This is the group's only coastal site and is attractively situated 300 m. from a fine sandy beach at the northern tip of the Ile d'Oléron. The nearest beach, the Plage des Huttes has been awarded the European Blue Flag accreditation for its cleanliness. The site is open all year and a new heated and covered swimming pool was recently added. The Ile d'Oléron has miles of excellent cycle tracks and a number of these run very close to the site. The 48 wooden chalets here are attractively dispersed around the site and are all available for rent.

Special offers

TV rental is included in chalet and mobile home rental prices.

You might like to know

The best way to explore the island is on two wheels with miles of cycle tracks and discounted bicycle hire on site.

- ☐ **Beach on site**
- ☑ **Beach within 1 km**
- ☑ **Sandy beach**
- ☑ **Blue Flag quality**
- ☑ **Lifeguard** *(high season)*
- ☐ **Sun lounger and/or deckchair hire**
- ☑ **Watersports** *(e.g. sailing or windsurfing)*
- ☑ **Snacks and drinks**
- ☐ **Sunshades/sunbeds**
- ☐ **Dogs allowed** *(on the beach)*

Facilities: No bar, restaurant or snack bar, but bread can be ordered. Ice-creams for sale. Swimming pool (9 x 5 m). Play area. Games room. Boules. Communal barbecue. Electric barbecues to hire. Chalets for rent. Security barrier. Off site: Nearest beach 300 m. Sailing and windsurfing. Fishing. Riding. Cycle and walking trails. Supermarket 6 km. St Denis d'Oléron with good shops and restaurants.

Open: All year.

Directions: Take exit 35 from the A10 motorway (Saintes) and then head west on the D728 to Marennes. Cross the bridge to the Ile d'Oléron and then follow the D26 and D734 to St Denis d'Oleron at the north of the island. Turn sharp left at 'Croustille Snack Bar' into rue St Denis signed Bétaudière. Follow this road for about 2 km. and at T junction, turn left and the site is on your left. GPS: 46.01355, -1.39182

Charges guide

Contact the site for details.

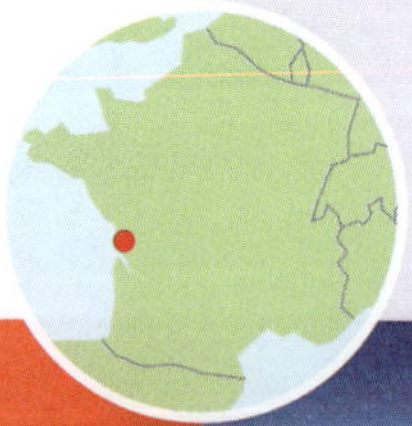

FRANCE – Alèria

Riva Bella Nature Resort & Spa

B.P. 21, F-20270 Alèria (Haute-Corse)
t: 04 95 38 81 10 e: rivabella.corsica@gmail.com
alanrogers.com/FR20040 www.rivabella-corsica.com

Accommodation: ☑ Pitch ☑ Mobile home/chalet ☐ Hotel/B&B ☐ Apartment

This is a relaxed, informal, spacious site alongside an extremely long and beautiful beach. Riva Bella is naturist from 16 May to 19 September only. It offers a variety of pitches situated in beautiful countryside and seaside. The site is divided into several areas with 200 pitches (133 for touring with 6A electricity), some of which are alongside the sandy beach with little shade. Others are in a shady wooded glade on the hillside. The huge fish-laden lakes are a fine feature of this site and a superb balnéotherapy centre offers the very latest beauty and relaxation treatments (men and women) based on marine techniques. The charming owner, Marie Claire Pasqual, is justifiably proud of the site and the fairly unobtrusive rules are designed to ensure that everyone is able to relax, whilst preserving the natural beauty of the environment. Cars are parked away from the pitches. The restaurant offers a sophisticated menu and the excellent beach restaurant/bar has superb sea views.

Special offers

For some accommodation rentals, a free ferry crossing to Corsica can be arranged.

You might like to know

Riva Bella was first opened over 40 years ago and maintains strong ecological interests, including making extensive use of local produce in the restaurant.

- ☑ Beach on site
- ☐ Beach within 1 km
- ☑ Sandy beach
- ☐ Blue Flag quality
- ☐ Lifeguard *(high season)*
- ☑ Sun lounger and/or deckchair hire
- ☐ Watersports *(e.g. sailing or windsurfing)*
- ☑ Snacks and drinks
- ☑ Sunshades/sunbeds
- ☑ Dogs allowed *(on the beach)*

Facilities: High standard toilet facilities. Provision for disabled visitors, children and babies. Laundry. Large shop (15/5-15/10). Fridge hire. Two restaurants with sea and lake views with reasonable prices. Excellent beach restaurant with bar. Watersports, sailing school, pedaloes, fishing. Balnéotherapy centre. Sauna. Aerobics. Giant chess. Archery. Fishing. Riding. Mountain bike hire. Half-court tennis. Walking with llamas. Internet. WiFi (charged). Professional evening entertainment programme. Off site: Tours of the island. Walking. Riding 7 km. Scuba diving 10 km. Paragliding.

Open: All year (naturist 16/5-19/9).

Directions: Site is 12 km. north of Aleria on N198 (Bastia) road. Watch for large signs and unmade road to site and follow for 4 km.
GPS: 42.16151, 9.55269

Charges guide

Per unit incl. 2 persons and electricity	€ 23,30 - € 40,30
extra person	€ 5,00 - € 9,00
child (3-8 yrs)	€ 2,00 - € 6,00
dog	€ 2,00 - € 3,50

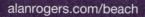

FRANCE – Bénodet

Camping du Letty

F-29950 Bénodet (Finistère)
t: 02 98 57 04 69 e: reception@campingduletty.com
alanrogers.com/FR29030 www.campingduletty.com

Accommodation: ☑ Pitch ☑ Mobile home/chalet ☐ Hotel/B&B ☐ Apartment

The Guyader family have ensured that this excellent and attractive site has plenty to offer for all the family. With a charming ambience, the site on the outskirts of the popular resort of Bénodet spreads over 22 acres with 493 pitches, all for touring units. Groups of four to eight pitches are set in cul-de-sacs with mature hedging and trees to divide each group. All pitches have electricity, water and drainage. As well as direct access to a small sandy beach, with a floating pontoon (safe bathing depends on the tides). The site is building a grand aquatic parc for 2011, with heated open air and indoor pools including children's pools, jacuzzi, slides etc. At the attractive floral entrance, former farm buildings provide a host of facilities including an extensively equipped fitness room and new 'wellness' rooms for massage and jacuzzis. There is also a modern, purpose built nightclub and bar providing high quality live entertainment most evenings (situated well away from most pitches to avoid disturbance).

You might like to know

Letty is beside 'la mer blanche', which empties and fills with the rhythm of the tides and is a haven for birds. The area is a paradise for walkers and nature lovers and has some wonderful sandy beaches.

☑ **Beach on site**
☐ **Beach within 1 km**
☑ **Sandy beach**
☐ **Blue Flag quality**
☐ **Lifeguard** *(high season)*
☐ **Sun lounger and/or deckchair hire**
☑ **Watersports**
(e.g. sailing or windsurfing)
☑ **Snacks and drinks**
☐ **Sunshades/sunbeds**
☑ **Dogs allowed** *(on the beach)*

Facilities: Six toilet blocks with mixed style WCs, washbasins in cabins and controllable hot showers (charged). Baby rooms. Facility for disabled visitors. Launderette. Hairdressing room. Motorcaravan service points. Well stocked shop. Snack bar and takeaway. Bar with games room and night club. Library with computers. Satellite TV. New swimming pool complex. Fitness centre. Saunas, jacuzzi and solarium (all charged). Tennis and squash (charged). Boules. Archery. Play area. Entertainment and activities (July/Aug). WiFi in reception. Off site: Sailing, fishing, riding and golf nearby.

Open: 11 June - 6 September.

Directions: From N165 take D70 Concarneau exit. At first roundabout take D44 to Fouesnant. Turn right at T-junction. After 2 km. turn left to Fouesnant (still D44). Continue through La Forêt Fouesnant and Fouesnant, picking up signs for Bénodet. Shortly before Bénodet at roundabout turn left (signed Le Letty). Turn right at next mini-roundabout and site is 500 m. on left.
GPS: 47.86700, -4.08783

Charges guide

Per unit incl. 2 persons and electricity	€ 20,50 - € 36,00
extra person	€ 4,00 - € 7,50
child (1-6 yrs)	€ 2,00 - € 3,75

FRANCE – Telgruc-sur-Mer

Camping le Panoramic

Route de la Plage-Penker, F-29560 Telgruc-sur-Mer (Finistère)
t: **02 98 27 78 41** e: **info@camping-panoramic.com**
alanrogers.com/FR29080 www.camping-panoramic.com

Accommodation: ☑ Pitch ☑ Mobile home/chalet ☐ Hotel/B&B ☐ Apartment

This medium sized, traditional site is situated on quite a steep, ten-acre hillside with fine views. It is personally run by M. Jacq and his family who all speak good English. The 200 pitches are arranged on flat, shady terraces, in small groups with hedges and flowering shrubs, and 20 pitches have services for motorcaravans. Divided into two parts, the main upper site is where most of the facilities are located, with the swimming pool, its terrace and a playground located with the lower pitches across the road. Some up-and-down walking is therefore necessary, but this is a small price to pay for such pleasant and comfortable surroundings. This area provides lovely coastal footpaths. The sandy beach and a sailing school at Trez-Bellec-Plage are a 700 m. walk. A Sites et Paysages member.

Special offers

Two people with a car, caravan, and 6A electricity = € 15/night (1/5-14/7, 21/8-15/9)

You might like to know

A stay at the Panoramic offers calm, relaxation and large pitches with beautiful views over the beach and the bay of Douarnenez.

- ☐ **Beach on site**
- ☑ **Beach within 1 km**
- ☑ **Sandy beach**
- ☐ **Blue Flag quality**
- ☐ **Lifeguard** *(high season)*
- ☐ **Sun lounger and/or deckchair hire**
- ☑ **Watersports** *(e.g. sailing or windsurfing)*
- ☑ **Snacks and drinks**
- ☐ **Sunshades/sunbeds**
- ☐ **Dogs allowed** *(on the beach)*

Facilities: The main site has two well kept toilet blocks with another very good block opened for main season across the road. All three include British and Turkish style WCs, washbasins in cubicles, facilities for disabled visitors, baby baths, plus laundry facilities. Motorcaravan services. Small shop (1/7-31/8). Refurbished bar/restaurant with takeaway (1/7-31/8). Barbecue area. Heated pool, paddling pool and jacuzzi (1/6-15/9). Playground. Games and TV rooms. Tennis. Bicycle hire. WiFi. Off site: Beach and fishing 700 m. Riding 6 km. Golf 14 km. Sailing school nearby.

Open: 1 May - 15 September.

Directions: Site is just south of Telgruc-sur-Mer. On D887 pass through Ste Marie du Ménez Horn. Turn left on D208 signed Telgruc-sur-Mer. Continue straight on through town and site is on right within 1 km. GPS: 48.22409, -4.37186

Charges guide

Per unit incl. 2 persons and electricity (10A)	€ 26,50
extra person	€ 5,00
child (under 7 yrs)	€ 3,00
dog	€ 2,00

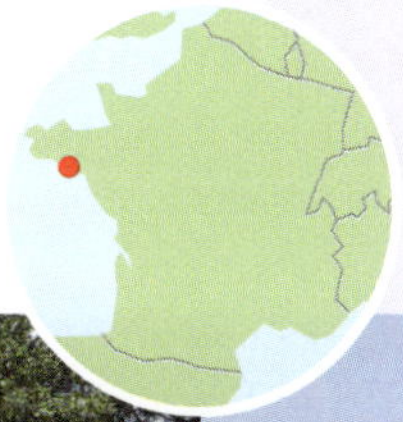

FRANCE – Névez

Camping le Raguénès-Plage

19 rue des Iles, F-29920 Névez (Finistère)
t: **02 98 06 80 69** e: **info@camping-le-raguenes-plage.com**
alanrogers.com/FR29090 **www.camping-le-raguenes-plage.com**

Accommodation: ☑ Pitch ☑ Mobile home/chalet ☐ Hotel/B&B ☐ Apartment

Mme. Guyader and her family will ensure you receive a warm welcome on arrival at this well kept and pleasant site. Le Raguénès-Plage is an attractive and well laid out site with many shrubs and trees. The 287 pitches are a good size, flat and grassy, separated by trees and hedges. All have electricity, water and drainage. The site is used by two tour operators (15 pitches), and has 61 mobile homes of its own. A pool complex complete with new heated indoor pool and water toboggan is a key feature and is close to the friendly bar, restaurant, shop and takeaway. From the far end of the campsite a delightful five minute walk along a path and through a cornfield takes you down to a pleasant, sandy beach looking out towards the Ile Verte and the Presqu'île de Raguénès.

You might like to know

There is a heated, covered pool, and a separate outdoor pool, also heated, with water slide and paddling pool.

- ☑ **Beach on site**
- ☐ **Beach within 1 km**
- ☑ **Sandy beach**
- ☑ **Blue Flag quality**
- ☐ **Lifeguard** *(high season)*
- ☐ **Sun lounger and/or deckchair hire**
- ☑ **Watersports** *(e.g. sailing or windsurfing)*
- ☑ **Snacks and drinks**
- ☐ **Sunshades/sunbeds**
- ☐ **Dogs allowed** *(on the beach)*

Facilities: Two clean, well maintained sanitary blocks include mixed style toilets, washbasins in cabins, baby baths and facilities for disabled visitors. Laundry room. Motorcaravan service point. Small shop (from 15/5). Bar and restaurant (from 1/6) with outside terrace and takeaway. Reading and TV room, Internet access point. Heated indoor and outdoor pools with sun terrace and paddling pool. Sauna (charged). Play areas. Games room. Various activities are organised in July/Aug. WiFi (charged).
Off site: Beach, fishing and watersports 300 m. Supermarket 3 km. Riding 4 km.

Open: 1 April - 30 September.

Directions: From N165 take D24 Kerampaou exit. After 3 km. turn right towards Nizon and bear right at church in village following signs to Névez (D77). Continue through Névez, following signs to Raguénès. Continue for 3 km. to site entrance on left (entrance is quite small and easy to miss). GPS: 47.79337, -3.80049

Charges guide

Per unit incl. 2 persons and electricity	€ 20,00 - € 35,90
extra person	€ 4,40 - € 6,00
child (under 7 yrs)	€ 2,20 - € 3,90
dog	€ 1,50 - € 3,20

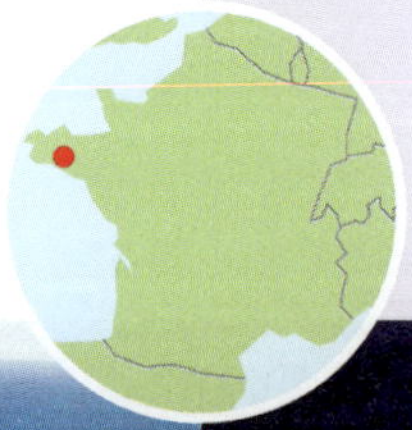

FRANCE – Landéda

Camping des Abers

Dunes de Sainte Marguerite, F-29870 Landéda (Finistère)
t: 02 98 04 93 35 e: camping-des-abers@wanadoo.fr
alanrogers.com/FR29130 www.camping-des-abers.com

Accommodation: ☑ Pitch ☑ Mobile home/chalet ☐ Hotel/B&B ☐ Apartment

This delightful 12-acre site is in a beautiful location almost at the tip of the Presqu'île Sainte Marguerite on the northwestern shores of Brittany. The peninsula lies between the mouths (abers) of two rivers, Aber Wrac'h and Aber Benoît. Camping des Abers is set just back from a wonderful sandy beach with rocky outcrops and islands you can walk to at low tide. There are 180 pitches, landscaped and terraced, some with amazing views, others sheltered by mature hedges, trees and flowering shrubs. This extensive site was created out of nothing by the le Cuff family who have tended it with loving care over the years. It is arranged on different levels avoiding any regimentation or crowding. Easily accessed by good internal roads, electricity is available to all (long leads may be needed). With its soft, white sandy beach the setting is ideal for those with younger children and this quiet, rural area provides a wonderful, tranquil escape from the hustle and bustle of life, even in high season.

You might like to know

There is a sailing club five minutes drive from the site, and on the nearby estuary there are oyster farms and a bird sanctuary.

- ☑ **Beach on site**
- ☐ **Beach within 1 km**
- ☑ **Sandy beach**
- ☐ **Blue Flag quality**
- ☐ **Lifeguard** *(high season)*
- ☐ **Sun lounger and/or deckchair hire**
- ☑ **Watersports** *(e.g. sailing or windsurfing)*
- ☐ **Snacks and drinks**
- ☐ **Sunshades/sunbeds**
- ☐ **Dogs allowed** *(on the beach)*

Facilities: Three toilet blocks, all refurbished are very clean and provide washbasins in cubicles and roomy showers. Good facilities for disabled visitors and babies. Laundry. Motorcaravan service point. Shop stocks essentials. Simple takeaway dishes (1/7-31/8). Play area. Games room. Hairdresser. Breton music and dancing. Cooking classes and guided walks arranged. Splendid beach with good bathing (best at high tide), fishing, windsurfing and other watersports. Long leads needed in places. Torch useful. Free internet and WiFi. Off site: Pizzeria next door. Tennis nearby. Sailing club 3 km. Riding 7 km. Golf 30 km. Miles of superb coastal walks.

Open: 28 April - 30 September.

Directions: Landéda is 55 km. west of Roscoff via D10 to Plougerneau then D13 crossing river bridge (Aber Wrac'h) and turning west to Lannilis. From N12 Morlaix-Brest road turn north on D59 to Lannilis. Continue through town taking road to Landéda, then follow signs for Dunes de Ste Marguerite, 'camping' and des Abers.
GPS: 48.59306, -4.60305

Charges guide

Per unit incl. 2 persons and electricity	€ 16,20 - € 18,00
extra person	€ 3,24 - € 3,60

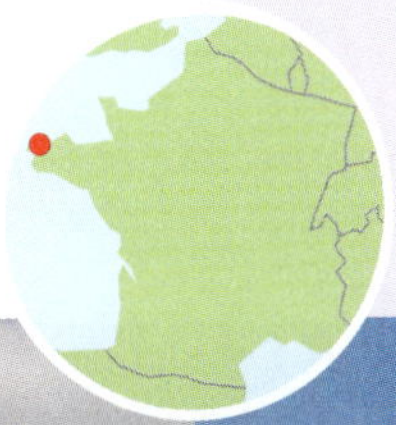

FRANCE – Saint Nic

Camping Domaine de Ker Ys

Pentrez-Plage, F-29550 Saint Nic (Finistère)
t: 02 98 26 53 95 e: camping-kerys@wanadoo.fr
alanrogers.com/FR29410 www.ker-ys.com

Accommodation: ☑ Pitch ☑ Mobile home/chalet ☐ Hotel/B&B ☐ Apartment

Camping De Ker Ys and Les Tamaris are adjacent sites that have been joined to form a camping village. Miles of wide sandy beach are just 20 m. away. The site has no bar or restaurant, but there is a bar next door and a snack stall in front of the site. The pool complex is very good with its slides, fountains and paddling pools. Entertainment such as karaoke and dance evenings are organised in high season. The 71 touring pitches vary in size and are divided by hedges. The site is now concentrating on the provision of mobile home holidays and touring visitors may feel overwhelmed by these. The close proximity of the superb beaches make this an ideal location for those who are keen on watersports where you can surf, paraglide and try your hand at sand sailing. St Nic is 2 km. away for supplies and perhaps a meal. Brest with its large port and the sealife centre, Oceanopolis, is a short drive away. There is an excellent motorway should you wish to visit some of the many sights and resorts in southern Brittany.

You might like to know

Locronan is one of Brittany's most picturesque villages and is often used as a film location. It makes a great day trip from this site.

- ☑ **Beach on site**
- ☐ **Beach within 1 km**
- ☑ **Sandy beach**
- ☐ **Blue Flag quality**
- ☑ **Lifeguard** *(high season)*
- ☐ **Sun lounger and/or deckchair hire**
- ☑ **Watersports** *(e.g. sailing or windsurfing)*
- ☑ **Snacks and drinks**
- ☐ **Sunshades/sunbeds**
- ☐ **Dogs allowed** *(on the beach)*

Facilities: Three unisex toilet blocks have British style toilets, showers and washbasins in cabins. Facilities for disabled visitors. Washing machines and dryers. Small shop. Swimming pool complex with slides, fountains and paddling pools. Play area. Mini-tennis. TV and games rooms. Beach 20 m. WiFi (charged). Off site: Beach 20 m. Shops, bars and restaurants nearby (but not many). Riding 15 km.

Open: 4 April - 19 September.

Directions: From the N165 (Quimper - Brest) take exit west at Châteaulin on D887 towards Crozon. Turn left to Saint Nic, then follow signs for Pentrez Plage and site. At the promenade turn left and site is 300 m. on the left.
GPS: 48.192161, -4.301303

Charges guide

Per unit incl. 1 or 2 persons	€ 15,00 - € 27,50
extra person	€ 2,50 - € 5,00
child (3-6 yrs)	€ 1,50 - € 4,00
dog	€ 2,00

FRANCE – Lesconil

Camping de la Grande Plage

71 rue Paul Langevin, F-29740 Lesconil (Finistère)
t: 02 98 87 88 27 e: contact@campinggrandeplage.com
alanrogers.com/FR29710 www.campinggrandeplage.com

Accommodation: ☑ Pitch ☑ Mobile home/chalet ☐ Hotel/B&B ☐ Apartment

Lesconil is a pleasant, traditional seaside resort, southwest of Quimper. La Grande Plage has direct access to an excellent sandy beach and is close to the village centre. There are 120 pitches here, most with electrical connections (3/6A), and a number of mobile homes and bungalow-style tents available for rent. Most pitches are well shaded. Leisure facilities include a recently constructed swimming pool with water slides and a separate paddling pool. A welcome drink is organised every week and other activities are on offer in high season, including themed meals and sports contests. The site's snack bar offers a range of hot and cold snacks. Lesconil has several good seafood restaurants, as well as plenty of shops. Running close to the site, the GR34 long distance footpath (sentier des douaniers) offers some superb coastal walking, stretching around the Breton coastline as far as Mont St Michel. Fishing is an important part of the local economy and the daily return of the fishing fleet is a colourful sight.

You might like to know

July and August feature a number of festivals and a 'Fez noz' (folklore evening). La Torche beach, popular with windsurfers and kitesurfers, is within 20 km.

- ☑ Beach on site
- ☐ Beach within 1 km
- ☑ Sandy beach
- ☐ Blue Flag quality
- ☐ Lifeguard *(high season)*
- ☐ Sun lounger and/or deckchair hire
- ☑ Watersports *(e.g. sailing or windsurfing)*
- ☑ Snacks and drinks
- ☑ Sunshades/sunbeds
- ☑ Dogs allowed *(on the beach)*

Facilities: Snack bar. Swimming pool complex with water slides and children's paddling pool. Play area. Tourist information. Accommodation for rent. Entertainment and activity programme. Off site: Cycle and walking tracks (including GR34 footpath). Fishing. Windsurfing. Golf. Quimper.

Open: 31 March - 31 October.

Directions: From Pont l'Abbé, head south on D2 and D102, passing through Plobannalec-Lesconil. Continue to Lesconil and follow signs to the site on Avenue Paul Langevin.
GPS: 47.7979, -4.22895

Charges guide

Per unit incl. 2 persons and electricity	€ 20,00
extra person	€ 4,90
child (under 7 yrs)	€ 2,55
dog	€ 1,90 - € 2,30

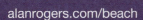

FRANCE – Hourtin-Plage

Airotel Camping la Côte d'Argent

F-33990 Hourtin-Plage (Gironde)
t: 05 56 09 10 25 e: info@cca33.com
alanrogers.com/FR33110 www.cca33.com

Accommodation: ☑ Pitch ☑ Mobile home/chalet ☑ Hotel/B&B ☐ Apartment

Côte d'Argent is a large, well equipped site for leisurely family holidays. It makes an ideal base for walkers and cyclists with over 100 km. of cycle lanes in the area. Hourtin-Plage is a pleasant invigorating resort on the Atlantic coast and a popular location for watersports enthusiasts. The site's top attraction is its pool complex, where wooden bridges connect the pools and islands and there are sunbathing and play areas plus an indoor heated pool. The site has 588 touring pitches (all with 10A electricity), not always clearly defined, arranged under trees with some on sand. High quality entertainment takes place at the impressive bar/restaurant near the entrance. Spread over 20 hectares of undulating sand-based terrain and in the midst of a pine forest. The site is well organised and ideal for children.

Special offers

Free admission to the large (3,500 sq.m) aquatic complex with heated, covered pool.

You might like to know

There is direct access from site to a network of 100 km. of cycle tracks. Nearby are the Médoc vineyards, the Arcachon Basin and the Gironde Estuary.

- ☐ **Beach on site**
- ☑ **Beach within 1 km**
- ☑ **Sandy beach**
- ☑ **Blue Flag quality**
- ☑ **Lifeguard** *(high season)*
- ☐ **Sun lounger and/or deckchair hire**
- ☑ **Watersports** *(e.g. sailing or windsurfing)*
- ☑ **Snacks and drinks**
- ☐ **Sunshades/sunbeds**
- ☑ **Dogs allowed** *(on the beach)*

Facilities: Very clean sanitary blocks include provision for disabled visitors. Washing machines. Motorcaravan service points. Large supermarket, restaurant, takeaway, pizzeria, bar (all open 1/6-15/9). Four outdoor pools with slides and flumes (1/6-19/9). Indoor pool (all season). Fitness room. Massage (Institut de Beauté). Tennis. Play areas. Miniclub, organised entertainment in season. Bicycle hire. WiFi (charged). ATM. Charcoal barbecues are not permitted. Hotel (12 rooms). Off site: Path to the beach 300 m. Fishing and riding. Golf 30 km.

Open: 14 May - 18 September.

Directions: Turn off D101 Hourtin-Soulac road 3 km. north of Hourtin. Then join D101E signed Hourtin-Plage. Site is 300 m. from the beach. GPS: 45.22297, -1.16465

Charges guide

Per unit incl. 2 persons and electricity	€ 26,00 - € 48,00
extra person	€ 4,00 - € 8,00
child (3-9 yrs)	€ 3,00 - € 7,00
dog	€ 2,00 - € 6,00

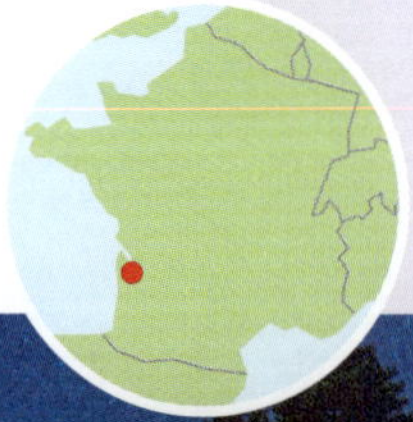

Yelloh! Village le Sérignan-Plage

Le Sérignan Plage, F-34410 Sérignan-Plage (Hérault)
t: 04 67 32 35 33 e: info@leserignanplage.com
alanrogers.com/FR34070 www.leserignanplage.com

Accommodation: ☑ Pitch ☑ Mobile home/chalet ☐ Hotel/B&B ☐ Apartment

With direct access onto a superb 600 m. sandy beach (including a naturist section) and with three swimming pools and another planned for next year, this is a must for a Mediterranean holiday. It is a friendly, family orientated site with perhaps the most comprehensive range of amenities we have come across. A collection of spa pools (balnéo) built in Romanesque style with colourful terracing and columns, overlooked by a very smart restaurant, Le Villa, is the 'pièce de résistance'. The balnéo spa is shared with the adjoining naturist site (under the same ownership). Having recently acquired an adjacent site, there are now over 1,000 pitches with 350 available for touring units and this is now a pretty large campsite. The touring pitches vary in size and in terms of shade. They are mainly on sandy soil and all have electricity. There are over 300 mobile homes and chalets to let, plus some 400 privately owned units. The heart of the site is a busy area with shops, a good restaurant, an indoor pool and a roof-top bar.

Special offers

Sunshine guarantee: in April, May and September, if the weather is poorer than expected, you can rearrange, shorten or cancel your holiday at no extra cost. You only pay for nights spent on site. Don't worry, though – it's always sunny in the south of France!

You might like to know

Yelloh! Village le Sérignan-Plage has a brilliant aqua complex with a lagoon style pool covering 850 sq.m, and a special covered pool for very young swimmers.

- ☑ **Beach on site**
- ☐ **Beach within 1 km**
- ☑ **Sandy beach**
- ☑ **Blue Flag quality**
- ☑ **Lifeguard** *(high season)*
- ☑ **Sun lounger and/or deckchair hire**
- ☑ **Watersports** *(e.g. sailing or windsurfing)*
- ☑ **Snacks and drinks**
- ☑ **Sunshades/sunbeds**
- ☐ **Dogs allowed** *(on the beach)*

Facilities: Several modern blocks with good facilities including showers with washbasin and WC. Facilities for disabled visitors. Baby bathroom. Launderette. Motorcaravan services. Supermarket, bakery and newsagent (all season). Other shops (21/4-2/10). ATM. Restaurants, bar and takeaway. Hairdresser. Balnéo spa. Gym. Heated indoor pool. Outdoor pools (21/4-2/10). Children's clubs. Evening entertainment. Sporting activities. Bicycle hire. Bus to Sérignan July/Aug. Beach (lifeguards 1/6-15/9). Off site: Riding 2 km. Golf 10 km. Sailing and windsurfing school on beach. Local markets.

Open: 21 April - 2 October.

Directions: From A9 exit 35 (Béziers Est) towards Sérignan, D64 (9 km). Before Sérignan, turn left, Sérignan-Plage (4 km). At small sign (blue) turn right. At T-junction turn left over small bridge and after left hand bend. Site is 100 m. GPS: 43.26308, 3.31976

Charges guide

Per unit incl. 2 persons and electricity	€ 15,00 - € 52,00
extra person	€ 5,00 - € 8,50
child (3-7 yrs)	free - € 8,50
dog	€ 4,00

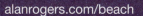

FRANCE – Marseillan-Plage

Camping la Creole

74 avenue des campings, F-34340 Marseillan-Plage (Hérault)
t: **04 67 21 92 69** e: **campinglacreole@wanadoo.fr**
alanrogers.com/FR34220 www.campinglacreole.com

Accommodation: ☑ Pitch ☑ Mobile home/chalet ☐ Hotel/B&B ☐ Apartment

This is a surprisingly tranquil, well cared for small campsite in the middle of this bustling resort that will appeal to those seeking a rather less frenetic ambience typical of many sites in this area. Essentially a family orientated site, it offers around 110 good sized, level, sandy pitches, all with 6A electricity and mostly with shade from trees and shrubs. There are also 15 mobile homes available to rent. It benefits from direct access to an extensive sandy beach (gated access) and the fact that there is no swimming pool or bar actually contributes to the tranquillity. It may even be seen as an advantage for families with younger children. The beach will be the main attraction here no doubt, and the town's extensive range of bars, restaurants and shops are all within a couple of minutes walk. It is well situated for visiting Sète, a miniature Venice, or Pézenas with an interesting history and lots of art and craft shops. Cap d'Agde, a modern resort with its large marina and super water park for children is popular.

You might like to know

Children can swim safely on the gently sloping beach with its fine sand. There is plenty of shade on the campsite, and all shops and services are less than 100 m. away.

- ☑ **Beach on site**
- ☐ **Beach within 1 km**
- ☑ **Sandy beach**
- ☑ **Blue Flag quality**
- ☑ **Lifeguard** *(high season)*
- ☐ **Sun lounger and/or deckchair hire**
- ☑ **Watersports** *(e.g. sailing or windsurfing)*
- ☑ **Snacks and drinks**
- ☐ **Sunshades/sunbeds**
- ☐ **Dogs allowed** *(on the beach)*

Facilities: Toilet facilities are in a traditional building, modernised inside to provide perfectly adequate, if not particularly luxurious, facilities including some washbasins in private cabins, a baby room and dog shower. Motorcaravan service point. Small play area. In high season beach games, dances, sangria evenings etc, are organised, all aimed particularly towards families. Communal barbecues only. WiFi. Off site: Local market day Tuesday. Bicycle hire outside site. Riding 1 km. Boat launching 1.5 km. Aqua park at Agde 5 km.

Open: 1 April - 15 October.

Directions: From A9 exit 34 take N312 towards Agde, then N112 towards Sète keeping a look out for signs to Marseillan-Plage off this road. Site is well signed in Marseillan-Plage.
GPS: 43.3206, 3.5501

Charges guide

Per unit incl. 2 persons and electricity	€ 16,30 - € 32,50
extra person (over 2 yrs)	€ 3,00 - € 6,00
dog	€ 2,00 - € 3,00

FRANCE – Cap d'Agde

Yelloh! Village Mer et Soleil

Chemin de Notre Dame à Saint Martin, Rochelongue, F-34300 Cap d'Agde (Hérault)
t: 04 67 94 21 14 e: contact@camping-mer-soleil.com
alanrogers.com/FR34290 www.camping-mer-soleil.com

Accommodation: ☑ Pitch ☑ Mobile home/chalet ☐ Hotel/B&B ☐ Apartment

Close to Cap d'Agde, this is a popular, well equipped site with many facilities. The pool area is particularly attractive with large palm trees, a whirlpool and slides, as well as a gym and wellness centre. An upstairs restaurant overlooks this area and the stage next to it. All ages are catered for and evening entertainment in July and August includes live shows. There are 477 pitches, around half taken by mobile homes and chalets (some to let, some privately owned). The touring pitches are hedged and have good shade from tall trees, all with 6A electricity. From the back of the site, a 1 km. long path leads to the white sandy beach at Rochelongue. A smart new reception has been built and a state-of-the-art balnéo can be found at the front of the site offering a wide range of treatments. It is open for public use with a 10% reduction offered to campers. The design inside is very impressive with a central grass area and fountain. The hydro pools are under a church-like roof with massage rooms, sauna and turkish bath to the sides.

You might like to know

Plage Rochelongue is the nearest beach, about 1 km away. Nearby are the popular resort of Cap d'Agde, the Camargue, the Canal du Midi and the vineyards of Languedoc Rousillon.

- ☐ Beach on site
- ☑ Beach within 1 km
- ☑ Sandy beach
- ☐ Blue Flag quality
- ☑ Lifeguard *(high season)*
- ☑ Sun lounger and/or deckchair hire
- ☑ Watersports *(e.g. sailing or windsurfing)*
- ☑ Snacks and drinks
- ☑ Sunshades/sunbeds
- ☐ Dogs allowed *(on the beach)*

Facilities: One large toilet block plus three smaller ones are fully equipped. Attractive units for children with small toilets, etc. Units for disabled visitors. Washing machine. Shop. Bar and restaurant. Heated swimming pools. Gym. State-of-the-art balnéo with hydro pools, massage rooms, sauna and turkish bath. Hairdresser. Play area. Tennis. Archery. Sporting activities and evening entertainment. Miniclub. WiFi. Off site: Sports and pool complex opposite site. Bus stop outside site. Beach and riding 1 km. Bezier airport within easy reach.

Open: 31 March - 6 October.

Directions: From A9 exit 34, follow N312 for Agde. It joins the N112 Béziers - Sète road. Cross bridge over Hérault river and turn right for Rochelongue. Turn left at next roundabout and site is a little further on the right.
GPS: 43.286183, 3.478

Charges guide

Per unit incl. 2 persons and electricity	€ 15,00 - € 44,00
extra person	€ 4,00 - € 8,00
child (3-7 yrs)	free - € 7,00
dog	€ 4,00

FRANCE – Valras-Plage

Camping Blue Bayou

Vendres Plage Ouest, F-34350 Valras-Plage (Hérault)
t: 04 67 37 41 97 e: infobluebayou@orange.fr
alanrogers.com/FR34370 www.bluebayou.fr

Accommodation: ☑ Pitch ☑ Mobile home/chalet ☐ Hotel/B&B ☐ Apartment

A pleasant site, Blue Bayou is situated at the far end of Vendres Plage near Le Grau Vendres (the port of Vendres). It is therefore in a much quieter location than many other sites, away from the more hectic, built-up areas of Vendres and Valras-Plage. The beach is 300 m. across sand dunes and there are open views from the site creating a feeling of spaciousness. There are 256 pitches, all with 10A electricity, with 74 privately owned mobile homes and 92 to let, including some chalets. The touring pitches are large, some with their own sanitary arrangements. Light shade is provided by a mixture of trees. The restaurant and bar area is very attractive, overlooking two swimming pools, one with a toboggan, joined by a bridge where lifeguards are posted. The owners and their family are proud of their site and you are made to feel very welcome. The site would be a good choice for couples and families, perhaps best visited outside the peak season, when it becomes very busy. In July and August a tourist train runs to link Valras and Vendres.

You might like to know

The site is just 300 m. from one of the most beautiful sandy beaches on the Mediterranean.

- ☑ **Beach on site**
- ☐ **Beach within 1 km**
- ☑ **Sandy beach**
- ☐ **Blue Flag quality**
- ☑ **Lifeguard** *(high season)*
- ☐ **Sun lounger and/or deckchair hire**
- ☑ **Watersports** *(e.g. sailing or windsurfing)*
- ☑ **Snacks and drinks**
- ☑ **Sunshades/sunbeds**
- ☑ **Dogs allowed** *(on the beach)*

Facilities: Individual toilet units for about half the touring pitches. Two separate blocks are fully equipped and are to be renovated. Baby bath and facilities for children. Facilities for disabled visitors. Laundry. Bar, restaurant and takeaway (open on demand in early season). Swimming pool (heated all season). Multisport court. Play area. Miniclub and entertainment in high season. WiFi throughout (charged). Off site: Fishing, boat launching and riding 1 km. Bicycle hire 3 km. Golf 25 km.

Open: 2 April - 24 September.

Directions: From A9 exit 36 (Béziers Ouest) follow directions for Valras-Plage and Vendres Plage over four roundabouts. At fifth roundabout (Port Conchylicole) follow sign for Vendres Plage Ouest and site is 500 m. on the left past the Ranch and tourist office. The entrance is quite tight. GPS: 43.227408, 3.243536

Charges guide

Per unit incl. 2 persons and electricity	€ 21,00 - € 47,00
incl. private sanitary facility	€ 25,00 - € 55,00
extra person (over 4 yrs)	€ 5,00 - € 9,00

FRANCE – Portiragnes-Plage

Camping les Sablons

Avenue des Muriers, F-34420 Portiragnes-Plage (Hérault)
t: 04 67 90 90 55 e: contact@les-sablons.com
alanrogers.com/FR34400 www.les-sablons.com

Accommodation: ☑ Pitch ☑ Mobile home/chalet ☐ Hotel/B&B ☐ Apartment

Les Sablons is an impressive and popular site with lots going on, a village in itself. Most of the facilities are arranged around the entrance with shops, a restaurant, a bar and a large pool complex with no less than five slides and three heated pools. There is also direct access to the white sandy beach at the back of the site close to a small lake. There is good shade on the majority of the site, although some of the newer touring pitches have less shade but are nearer the gate to the beach. On level sandy grass, all have 6A electricity. Of the 800 pitches, around half are taken by a range of mobile homes and chalets (many for hire, and a few for use by tour operators). It is possible to book a wide range of sporting, cultural and musical events as well as excursions. Children's clubs and evening entertainment is organised, in fact, this is a real holiday venue aiming to keep all the family happy. Some visitors simply stay on the site for their entire holiday – it certainly has everything. The site is very convenient for Beziers airport.

You might like to know

The site has direct access to the beach and dunes (closed 23.00-07.00). There is also a lake with hides for birdwatching.

- ☑ Beach on site
- ☐ Beach within 1 km
- ☑ Sandy beach
- ☑ Blue Flag quality
- ☐ Lifeguard *(high season)*
- ☐ Sun lounger and/or deckchair hire
- ☑ Watersports *(e.g. sailing or windsurfing)*
- ☐ Snacks and drinks
- ☐ Sunshades/sunbeds
- ☐ Dogs allowed *(on the beach)*

Facilities: Well equipped, modernised toilet blocks include large showers, some with washbasins. Baby baths and facilities for disabled visitors. Supermarket, bakery and newsagent. Bar, restaurant and takeaway. Swimming pool complex. Entertainment and activity programme with sports, music and cultural activities. Beach club. Children's club. Tennis. Archery. Play areas. Electronic games. ATM. Internet access. WiFi throughout site. Off site: Village and bicycle hire 100 m. Beach and riding 200 m. Canal du Midi 1 km. Parc Adventure (high wire adventure park) 1.5 km.

Open: 1 April - 30 September.

Directions: From A9 exit 35 (Béziers Est) follow signs for Vias and Agde (N112). After large roundabout pass exit to Cers then take exit for Portiragnes (D37). Follow for about 5 km. and pass over Canal du Midi towards Portiragnes-Plage. Site is on left after roundabout.
GPS: 43.28003, 3.36396

Charges guide

Per unit incl. 2 persons and electricity	€ 19,00 - € 48,00
extra person	€ 6,00 - € 10,00
child (acc. to age)	free - € 8,00
dog	€ 4,00

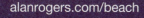

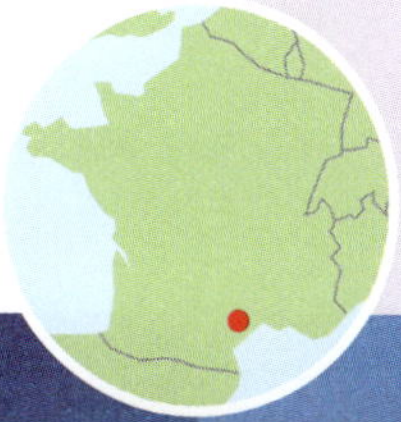

FRANCE – Vielle-Saint-Girons

Camping Club International Eurosol

Route de la Plage, F-40560 Vielle-Saint-Girons (Landes)
t: 05 58 47 90 14 e: contact@camping-eurosol.com
alanrogers.com/FR40060 www.camping-eurosol.com

Accommodation: ☑ Pitch ☑ Mobile home/chalet ☐ Hotel/B&B ☐ Apartment

Eurosol is an attractive, friendly and well maintained site extending over 15 hectares of undulating ground amongst mature pine trees giving good shade. Of the 356 touring pitches, 209 have electricity (10A) with 120 fully serviced. A wide range of mobile homes and chalets are available for rent too. This is very much a family site with multilingual entertainers. Many games and tournaments are organised and a beach volleyball competition is held regularly in front of the bar. The adjacent boules terrain is also floodlit. An excellent sandy beach 700 m. from the site has supervised bathing in high season, and is ideal for surfing. The swimming pool complex is impressive with three large pools, one covered and heated, and a large children's paddling pool. There is a convivial restaurant and takeaway food service. A large supermarket is well stocked with fresh bread daily and international newspapers. Cycle trails lead from the site through the vast forests of Les Landes, and a riding centre is located just 100 m. away.

You might like to know

A quiet, very high quality camping village in the shade of the pine forest, and a great spot for unforgettable family holidays.

- ☐ Beach on site
- ☑ Beach within 1 km
- ☑ Sandy beach
- ☐ Blue Flag quality
- ☑ Lifeguard *(high season)*
- ☐ Sun lounger and/or deckchair hire
- ☑ Watersports *(e.g. sailing or windsurfing)*
- ☑ Snacks and drinks
- ☐ Sunshades/sunbeds
- ☑ Dogs allowed *(on the beach)*

Facilities: Four main toilet blocks and two smaller blocks are comfortable and clean with facilities for babies and disabled visitors. Motorcaravan services. Fridge rental. Well stocked shop and bar (all season). Restaurant, takeaway (2/6-8/9). Stage for live shows (July/Aug). Outdoor swimming pool, paddling pool and heated covered pool (all season). Tennis. Multisports court. Bicycle hire. WiFi (charged). Charcoal barbecues are not permitted. Off site: Riding (July/Aug) 200 m. Surf school 500 m. Beach and fishing 700 m. Golf 18 km.

Open: 19 May - 15 September.

Directions: Turn off D652 at St Girons on D42 towards St Girons-Plage. Site is on left before coming to beach (4.5 km).
GPS: 43.95166, -1.35212

Charges guide

Per unit incl. 2 persons and electricity	€ 18,00 - € 35,00
extra person (over 4 yrs)	€ 5,00
dog	€ 4,00

FRANCE – Mimizan

Airotel Club Marina-Landes

Rue Marina, F-40200 Mimizan (Landes)
t: **05 58 09 12 66** e: **contact@clubmarina.com**
alanrogers.com/FR40080 www.marinalandes.com

Accommodation: ☑ Pitch ☑ Mobile home/chalet ☐ Hotel/B&B ☐ Apartment

Well maintained and clean, with helpful staff, Club Marina-Landes would be a very good choice for a family holiday. Activities include discos, play groups for children, specially trained staff to entertain teenagers and concerts for more mature campers. There are numerous sports opportunities and a superb sandy beach nearby. A nightly curfew ensures that all have a good night's sleep. A new leisure pool is planned for 2012. The site has 401 touring pitches (316 with 10A electricity) and 135 mobile homes and chalets for rent. The pitches are on firm grass, most with hedges and they are large (mostly 100 sq.m. or larger). If ever a campsite could be said to have two separate identities, then Club Marina-Landes is surely the one. In early and late season it is quiet, with the pace of life in low gear – come July and until 1 September, all the facilities are open and there is fun for all the family with the chance that family members will only meet together at meal times.

You might like to know

Why not take the Mailloueyre lake trail (1 km, 15 minutes on foot)? The area is officially classified as a nature reserve and is a delight for botanists and nature lovers alike.

- ☐ **Beach on site**
- ☑ **Beach within 1 km**
- ☑ **Sandy beach**
- ☐ **Blue Flag quality**
- ☑ **Lifeguard** *(high season)*
- ☐ **Sun lounger and/or deckchair hire**
- ☑ **Watersports** *(e.g. sailing or windsurfing)*
- ☑ **Snacks and drinks**
- ☐ **Sunshades/sunbeds**
- ☑ **Dogs allowed** *(on the beach)*

Facilities: Five toilet blocks (opened as required), well maintained with showers and many washbasins in cabins. Facilities for babies, children and disabled visitors. Laundry facilities. Motorcaravan services. Fridge hire. Shop (freshly baked bread) and bar (30/4-10/9). Restaurant, snack bar, pizzas and takeaway (1/5-10/9). Covered pool and outdoor pools (30/4-13/9). Minigolf. Tennis. Bicycle hire. Play area. Entertainment and activities (high season). Gas or electric barbecues only. WiFi (charged). Off site: Beach and fishing 500 m. Bus service and riding 1 km. Golf 8 km. Mimizan 8 km.

Open: 30 April - 13 September.

Directions: Heading west from Mimizan centre, take D626 passing Abbey Museum. Straight on at lights (crossing D87/D67). Next lights turn left. After 2 km. at T-junction turn left. Follow signs to site. GPS: 44.20447, -1.29099

Charges guide

Per unit incl. 3 persons and electricity	€ 18,00 - € 49,00
extra person	€ 4,00 - € 10,00
child (3-13 yrs)	€ 3,00 - € 8,00
dog	€ 2,00 - € 5,00

FRANCE – Biscarrosse

Camping du Domaine de la Rive

Route de Bordeaux, F-40600 Biscarrosse (Landes)
t: **05 58 78 12 33** e: **info@lafive.fr**
alanrogers.com/FR40100 www.larive.fr

Accommodation: ☑ Pitch ☑ Mobile home/chalet ☐ Hotel/B&B ☐ Apartment

Surrounded by pine woods, la Rive has a superb beach-side location on Lac de Sanguinet. It provides 250 mostly level, numbered and clearly defined touring pitches of 100 sq.m. all with electricity connections (10A). The swimming pool complex is wonderful with pools linked by water channels and bridges. There is also a jacuzzi, paddling pool and two large swimming pools all surrounded by sunbathing areas and decorated with palm trees. An indoor pool is heated and open all season. This is a friendly site with a good mix of nationalities. The latest additions are a super children's aquapark with various games, and a top quality bar/restaurant complex where regular entertainment is organised. The beach is excellent, shelving gently to provide safe bathing for all ages. There are windsurfers and small craft can be launched from the site's slipway.

You might like to know

The lakeside beach offers many watersports including catamaran sailing, rowing and canoeing and, on Monday to Thursday afternoons, jet skiing.

- ☑ **Beach on site**
- ☐ **Beach within 1 km**
- ☑ **Sandy beach**
- ☐ **Blue Flag quality**
- ☐ **Lifeguard** *(high season)*
- ☐ **Sun lounger and/or deckchair hire**
- ☑ **Watersports** *(e.g. sailing or windsurfing)*
- ☐ **Snacks and drinks**
- ☐ **Sunshades/sunbeds**
- ☐ **Dogs allowed** *(on the beach)*

Facilities: Five good clean toilet blocks have washbasins in cabins and mainly British style toilets. Facilities for disabled visitors. Baby baths. Motorcaravan service point. Shop with gas. New bar/restaurant complex with entertainment. Swimming pool complex (supervised July/Aug). Games room. Play area. Tennis. Bicycle hire. Boules. Archery. Fishing. Waterskiing. Watersports equipment hire. Tournaments (June-Aug). Skateboard park. Trampolines. Miniclub. No charcoal barbecues on pitches. WiFi (charged). Off site: Riding 2 km. Golf 8 km. Beach 17 km.

Open: 6 April - 9 September.

Directions: Take D652 from Sanguinet to Biscarrosse and site is signed on the right in about 6 km. Turn right and follow tarmac road for 2 km. GPS: 44.46052, -1.13065

Charges guide

Per unit incl. 2 persons and electricity	€ 24,50 - € 47,00
extra person	€ 3,80 - € 8,50
child (3-7 yrs)	€ 2,50 - € 7,00
dog	€ 5,00 - € 7,00

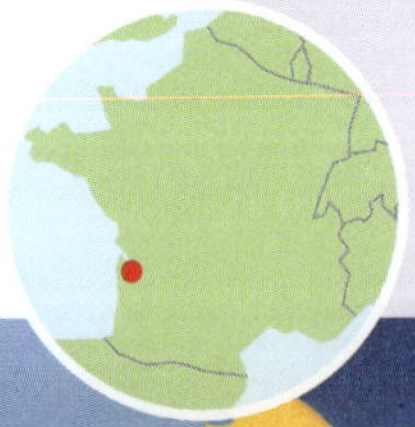

FRANCE – Messanges

Airotel le Vieux Port

Plage Sud, F-40660 Messanges (Landes)
t: 01 76 76 70 00 e: contact@levieuxport.com
alanrogers.com/FR40180 www.levieuxport.com

Accommodation: ☑ Pitch ☑ Mobile home/chalet ☐ Hotel/B&B ☐ Apartment

A well established destination appealing particularly to families with teenage children, this lively site has 1,546 pitches of mixed sizes, most with electricity (6A). The camping area is well shaded by pines and pitches are generally of a good size, attractively grouped around the toilet blocks. There are many tour operators here and well over a third of the site is taken up with mobile homes and chalets. An enormous 7,000 sq.m. aquatic park is now open, the largest on any French campsite. This heated complex is exceptional, boasting five outdoor pools, three large water slides plus waves and heated spa. There is also a heated indoor pool. The area to the north of Bayonne is heavily forested and a number of very large campsites are located close to the superb Atlantic beaches. Le Vieux Port is probably the largest, and certainly one of the most impressive, of these. At the back of the site a path leads across the dunes to a good beach (400 m). Other recent innovations include an outdoor fitness area and a superb riding centre.

Special offers

Special offers on accommodation rentals. Programme of activities and entertainment in July and August.

You might like to know

Le Vieux Port is very close to both the Basque Country and Spain (only 70 km. away). There are numerous activities on offer – why not try something completely new? Don't forget to try the varied local gastronomy.

- ☐ Beach on site
- ☑ Beach within 1 km
- ☑ Sandy beach
- ☐ Blue Flag quality
- ☑ Lifeguard *(high season)*
- ☐ Sun lounger and/or deckchair hire
- ☑ Watersports *(e.g. sailing or windsurfing)*
- ☑ Snacks and drinks
- ☑ Sunshades/sunbeds
- ☑ Dogs allowed *(on the beach)*

Facilities: Nine well appointed, recently renovated toilet blocks with facilities for disabled visitors. Motorcaravan services. Good supermarket and various smaller shops in high season. Several restaurants, takeaway and three bars (all open all season). Large pool complex (no Bermuda shorts; open all season) including new covered pool and Polynesian themed bar. Tennis. Multisport pitch. Minigolf. Outdoor fitness area. Fishing. Bicycle hire. Riding centre. Organised activities in high season including frequent discos and karaoke evenings. Only communal barbecues are allowed. WiFi (charged). Off site: Beach 400 m. Sailing 2 km. Golf 8 km.

Open: 31 March - 30 September.

Directions: Leave RN10 at Magescq exit heading for Soustons. Pass through Soustons following signs for Vieux-Boucau. Bypass this town and site is clearly signed to the left at second roundabout. GPS: 43.79778, -1.40111

Charges guide

Per unit incl. 2 persons and electricity	€ 21,30 - € 61,00
extra person	€ 4,80 - € 9,00
child (under 13 yrs)	€ 3,80 - € 6,20
dog	€ 3,10 - € 5,80

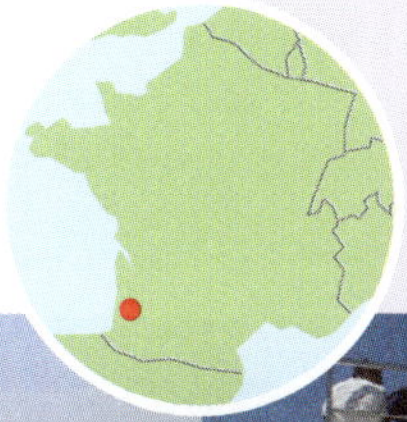

FRANCE – Moliets-Plage

Le Saint-Martin Camping

Avenue de l'Océan, F-40660 Moliets-Plage (Landes)
t: **05 58 48 52 30** e: **contact@camping-saint-martin.fr**
alanrogers.com/FR40190 www.camping-saint-martin.fr

Accommodation: ☑ Pitch ☑ Mobile home/chalet ☐ Hotel/B&B ☐ Apartment

A family site aimed mainly at couples and young families, St-Martin is a welcome change from most of the sites in this area in that it has only a relatively small number of mobile homes (127) compared to the number of touring pitches (383). First impressions are of a neat, tidy, well cared for site and the direct access to a wonderful fine sandy beach is an added bonus. The pitches are mainly typically French in style with low hedges separating them, and with some shade. Electricity hook ups are 10-15A and a number of pitches also have water and drainage. Entertainment in high season is low key (with the emphasis on quiet nights) – daytime competitions and a miniclub, plus the occasional evening entertainment, well away from the pitches and with no discos or karaoke. With pleasant chalets and mobile homes to rent, a top-class pool complex and an 18-hole golf course 700 m. away (special rates negotiated), this would be an ideal destination for a golfing weekend or a longer stay.

You might like to know

Courant d'Huchet, a conservation area, is delightful and has a number of walks and some beautiful views.

- ☑ **Beach on site**
- ☐ **Beach within 1 km**
- ☑ **Sandy beach**
- ☑ **Blue Flag quality**
- ☑ **Lifeguard** *(high season)*
- ☐ **Sun lounger and/or deckchair hire**
- ☑ **Watersports** *(e.g. sailing or windsurfing)*
- ☐ **Snacks and drinks**
- ☐ **Sunshades/sunbeds**
- ☑ **Dogs allowed** *(on the beach)*

Facilities: Seven toilet blocks of a high standard and very well maintained, have washbasins in cabins, large showers, baby rooms and facilities for disabled visitors. Motorcaravan service point. Washing machines and dryers. Fridge rental. Supermarket. Bars, restaurants and takeaways. Indoor pool, jacuzzi and sauna (charged July/Aug). Outdoor pool area with jacuzzi and paddling pool (15/6-15/9). Multisport pitch. Play area. Bicycle hire. Beach access. Internet access. Electric barbecues only. Off site: Fishing and beach 300 m. Golf and tennis 700 m. Sailing 6 km. Riding 8 km.

Open: 4 April - 7 November.

Directions: From the N10 take D142 to Lèon, then D652 to Moliets-et-Mar. Follow signs to Moliets-Plage, site is well signed.
GPS: 43.85242, -1.38732

Charges guide

Per unit incl. 2 persons and electricity	€ 22,70 - € 48,60
extra person	€ 6,00 - € 7,50
child (under 10 yrs)	€ 4,00 - € 5,30
dog	free - € 5,00

Prices are for reserved pitches.

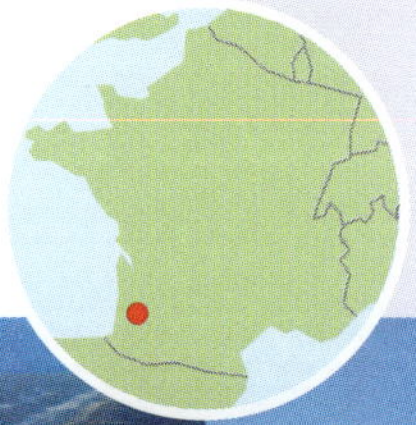

FRANCE – La Baule

Camping les Ajoncs d'Or

Chemin du Rocher, F-44500 La Baule (Loire-Atlantique)
t: 02 40 60 33 29 e: contact@ajoncs.com
alanrogers.com/FR44170 www.ajoncs.com

Accommodation: ☑ Pitch ☑ Mobile home/chalet ☐ Hotel/B&B ☐ Apartment

This site is situated in pine woods on the inland side of la Baule and its beautiful bay. A well maintained, natural woodland setting provides a wide variety of pitch types (just over 200), some level and bordered with hedges and tall trees to provide shade and many others that maintain the natural characteristics of the woodland. Most pitches have electricity and water nearby and are usually of a larger size. A central building provides a shop and an open friendly bar that serves snacks and takeaways. The new English speaking owner has extensive plans for this campsite. Large areas of woodland have been retained for quiet and recreational purposes and are safe for children to roam. It can be difficult to find an informal campsite close to an exciting seaside resort that retains its touring and camping identity, but les Ajoncs d'Or does this. Enjoy the gentle breezes off the sea that constantly rustle the trees. The family are justifiably proud of their site.

You might like to know

There are plenty of activities on offer including a children's club, special events and a choice of beaches within 20 km.

- ☐ Beach on site
- ☑ Beach within 1 km
- ☑ Sandy beach
- ☑ Blue Flag quality
- ☑ Lifeguard *(high season)*
- ☑ Sun lounger and/or deckchair hire
- ☑ Watersports *(e.g. sailing or windsurfing)*
- ☑ Snacks and drinks
- ☑ Sunshades/sunbeds
- ☐ Dogs allowed *(on the beach)*

Facilities: Two good quality sanitary blocks are clean and well maintained providing plenty of facilities including a baby room. Washing machines and dryers. Shop and bar (July/Aug). Snack bar (July/Aug). Good size swimming pool and paddling pool (1/6-5/9). Sports and playground areas. Bicycle hire. Reception with security barrier (closed 22.30-07.30). Off site: Everything for an enjoyable holiday can be found in nearby la Baule. Beach, fishing and riding 1.5 km. Golf 3 km.

Open: 1 April - 30 October.

Directions: From N171 take exit for La Baule les Pins. Follow signs for 'La Baule Centre', then left at roundabout in front of Carrefour supermarket and follow site signs. GPS: 47.28950, -2.37367

Charges guide

Per unit incl. 2 persons and electricity	€ 18,00 - € 30,00
extra person	€ 4,20 - € 7,00
child (2-7 yrs)	€ 2,10 - € 3,50
dog	€ 1,20 - € 2,00

FRANCE – Ravenoville Plage

Kawan Village le Cormoran

2 le Cormoran, F-50480 Ravenoville Plage (Manche)
t: **02 33 41 33 94** e: **lecormoran@wanadoo.fr**
alanrogers.com/FR50050 www.lecormoran.com

Accommodation: ☑ Pitch ☑ Mobile home/chalet ☐ Hotel/B&B ☐ Apartment

This welcoming, environmentally friendly, family run site, close to Cherbourg and Caen, is situated just across the road from a long sandy beach. It is also close to Utah beach and is ideally located for those wishing to visit the many museums, landing beaches and remembrance gardens of WW2. On flat, quite open ground, the site has 110 good size pitches on level grass, all with 6/10A electricity (Europlug). Some extra large pitches are available. The well kept pitches are separated by mature hedges and the site is decorated with flowering shrubs. A covered pool, a sauna and a gym are among recent improvements. These facilities, plus a shop, comfortable bar and takeaway are open all season. This modern, clean and fresh looking campsite caters for both families and couples and would be ideal for a holiday in this interesting area of France. The country roads provide opportunities for exploring on foot or by bike. There are many small towns in the area and in early June historical groups often re-enact the events of 1944-1945.

You might like to know

The campsite is on the Normandy landing beaches with their many museums and bunkers. In July and August you can go riding from the site along the wide stretches of sand.

- ☑ **Beach on site**
- ☐ **Beach within 1 km**
- ☑ **Sandy beach**
- ☐ **Blue Flag quality**
- ☐ **Lifeguard** *(high season)*
- ☐ **Sun lounger and/or deckchair hire**
- ☑ **Watersports** *(e.g. sailing or windsurfing)*
- ☐ **Snacks and drinks**
- ☐ **Sunshades/sunbeds**
- ☑ **Dogs allowed** *(on the beach)*

Facilities: Four toilet blocks, three heated, are maintained to a good standard. Laundry facilities. Shop. Bar and terrace. Snacks and takeaway. Outdoor pool (1/6-15/9, unsupervised). New covered pool, sauna and gym (all season). Play areas. Tennis. Boules. Entertainment, TV and games room. Billiard golf. Archery (July/Aug). Hairdresser and masseuse. Bicycle and shrimp net hire. Riding (July/Aug). Communal barbecues. BMX park for children. WiFi (charged).
Off site: Beach 20 m. Sand yachting. Golf (9 holes) 3 km. Ste-Mère-Eglise with annual D-Day celebrations in June 9 km.

Open: 7 April - 29 September.

Directions: From N13 take Ste Mère-Eglise exit and in centre of town take road to Ravenoville (6 km), then Ravenoville-Plage (3 km). Just before beach turn right and site is 500 m.
GPS: 49.46643, -1.23533

Charges guide

Per unit incl. 2 persons and electricity	€ 21,00 - € 33,00
extra person	€ 4,00 - € 7,90
child (5-10 yrs)	€ 2,00 - € 3,00

FRANCE – Pénestin-sur-Mer

Camping des Iles

La Pointe du Bile, B.P. 4, F-56760 Pénestin-sur-Mer (Morbihan)
t: 02 99 90 30 24 e: contact@camping-des-iles.fr
alanrogers.com/FR56120 www.camping-des-iles.fr

Accommodation: ☑ Pitch ☑ Mobile home/chalet ☐ Hotel/B&B ☐ Apartment

You will receive a warm, friendly welcome at this family run campsite. The owner, Madame Communal, encourages everyone to make the most of this beautiful region. Of the 184 pitches, 103 are for touring. Most are flat, hedged and of a reasonable size (larger caravans and American motorhomes are advised to book) and all have electricity. Some pitches have sea views and overlook the beach. There is direct access to cliff-top walks and local beaches (you can even walk to small off-shore islands at low tide). The attractive heated swimming pool complex provides a focal point for all ages. Most pitches for mobile homes and chalets are in a separate site across the road. Ideally placed with a ramp for launching small boats and sea fishing, although the tide does go out a long way.

You might like to know

It's well worth taking part in one of the free 'Découverte du Littoral' guided walks, with an opportunity to collect and taste some seafood and maybe capture the stunning sunset on film!

- ☑ Beach on site
- ☐ Beach within 1 km
- ☑ Sandy beach
- ☑ Blue Flag quality
- ☑ Lifeguard *(high season)*
- ☐ Sun lounger and/or deckchair hire
- ☑ Watersports *(e.g. sailing or windsurfing)*
- ☐ Snacks and drinks
- ☐ Sunshades/sunbeds
- ☐ Dogs allowed *(on the beach)*

Facilities: The new large central toilet block is spotlessly clean with washbasins in cabins and showers. Laundry facilities. Facilities for disabled visitors, and baby room. Shop (all season). Bar and restaurant with takeaway (15/5-15/9). Pool complex (15/5-30/9). Bicycle hire. Activities and entertainment in July/Aug. Riding. Across the road in Parc des Iles (mobile home section of site): TV room, multisports pitch, tennis court and motorcaravan service point. No electric barbecues. Internet access in bar (charged). Off site: Windsurfing 500 m. Sailing school 3 km. Golf 20 km.

Open: 2 April - 17 October.

Directions: From D34 (La Roche-Bernard), at roundabout just after entering Pénestin take D201 south (Assérac). Take right fork to Pointe-du-Bile after 2 km. Turn right at crossroads just before beach. Site is on left.
GPS: 47.44543, -2.48396

Charges guide

Per unit incl. 2 persons and electricity	€ 20,50 - € 39,50
extra person (over 7 yrs)	€ 2,30 - € 5,80
child (0-7 yrs)	free - € 3,20
dog	€ 2,00 - € 4,00

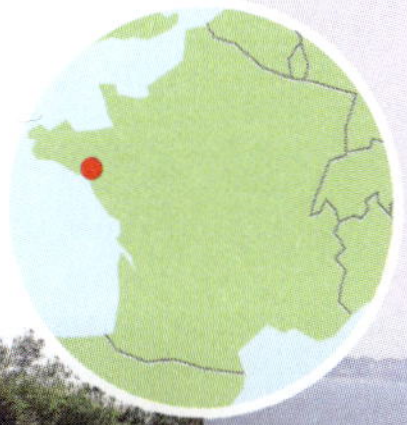

FRANCE – Carnac

Camping le Dolmen

Chemin de Beaumer, F-56340 Carnac (Morbihan)
t: **02 97 52 12 35** e: **camping.ledolmen@gmail.com**
alanrogers.com/FR56510 www.campingledolmen.com

Accommodation: ☑ Pitch ☑ Mobile home/chalet ☐ Hotel/B&B ☐ Apartment

Le Dolmen is a family site located on the eastern edge of Carnac. The site has 130 pitches, of which around 70 are available to tourers. Other pitches are taken by mobile homes (around 12 are to rent). Pitches are of a good size and are mostly equipped with electricity. A number of pitches outside the main gate in a parking area have been specially equipped for motorcaravans (with services). On-site amenities include a small snack bar and a swimming pool. The nearest beach, le Men Dû, is around 600 m. away. It is a particularly attractive beach, shelving gently and with crystal waters. Carnac needs little introduction and is best known for its alignments of more than 3,000 prehistoric standing stones. In high season, Carnac-Plage is quite different from the old town, with many lively bars and night clubs. To the east, la Trinité-sur-Mer is one of Brittany's premier sailing resorts and has many attractive restaurants. To the south, Quiberon retains a character all of its own with an important fishing tradition.

You might like to know

A marina and a yacht club can be found in Carnac, near Quiberon, with sailings to Belle-Ile-en-Mer. The rugged coastline here will appeal to lovers of the seashore. There is a children's club on site.

☐ **Beach on site**
☑ **Beach within 1 km**
☑ **Sandy beach**
☐ **Blue Flag quality**
☑ **Lifeguard** *(high season)*
☐ **Sun lounger and/or deckchair hire**
☐ **Watersports** *(e.g. sailing or windsurfing)*
☑ **Snacks and drinks**
☑ **Sunshades/sunbeds**
☑ **Dogs allowed** *(on the beach)*

Facilities: Two toilet blocks (one due for total refurbishment ahead of the 2012 season). Snack bar. Morning bread service. Heated swimming pool (1/6-31/8). Play area. Volleyball. Activity and entertainment programme. Motorcaravan services. WiFi in some areas (charged). Mobile homes for rent. Off site: Nearest beach 600 m. Fishing and bicycle hire 1 km. Sailing 1 km. Riding 3 km.

Open: 1 April - 11 September.

Directions: Approaching from the north (Auray) take D768 towards Quiberon and then D119 to Carnac. Upon arriving in Carnac, follow signs to Carnac-Plage and then to La Trinité-sur-Mer using D186 (Avenue des Druides). The site is clearly indicated to the left, on the edge of the town. GPS: 47.58076, -3.05751

Charges guide

Per unit incl. 2 persons and electricity	€ 21,50 - € 32,50
extra person	€ 4,30 - € 7,00
child (under 7 yrs)	€ 2,80 - € 4,00
dog	€ 2,10

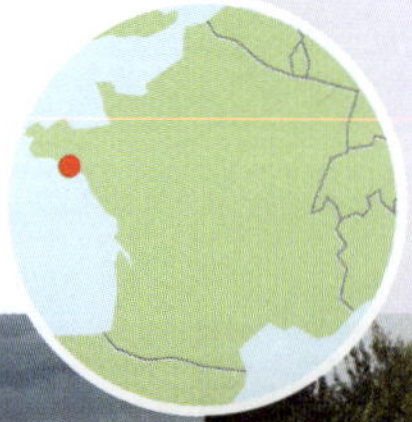

FRANCE – Quiberon

Camping Bois d'Amour

87, rue St Clement, F-56170 Quiberon (Morbihan)
t: 02 97 50 13 52 e: boisdamour@hotmail.com
alanrogers.com/FR56520 www.homair.com

Accommodation: ☑ Pitch ☑ Mobile home/chalet ☐ Hotel/B&B ☐ Apartment

Le Bois d'Amour faces toward Belle Ile and lies just 150 m. from the attractive, sandy Goviro beach at the southern end of the Quiberon peninsula. There are 290 pitches here, of which around 110 are for touring units, most with electricity. Other pitches are occupied by mobile homes and chalets (available for rent). On-site amenities include a large outdoor pool and a separate children's pool. Quiberon is explored by bicycle and these are available to rent on site. In high season, a regular programme of activities and entertainment is organised, including activities for children. Thalassotherapy is very popular in this region and specialist centres are available at both Quiberon and nearby Carnac. Quiberon is otherwise renowned for its sardine production, the origins of which date back to the early 19th century. Nowadays, it is home to many excellent seafood restaurants and tourism has long since replaced fishing as the primary activity. Belle Ile lies 14 km. to the south of Quiberon and is the largest island off the Breton coast.

You might like to know

It is well worth watching the fishing fleet return to Loctudy every day (around 4.30 pm). You can't get fresher fish for the barbecue.

- ☐ Beach on site
- ☑ Beach within 1 km
- ☑ Sandy beach
- ☐ Blue Flag quality
- ☐ Lifeguard *(high season)*
- ☐ Sun lounger and/or deckchair hire
- ☑ Watersports *(e.g. sailing or windsurfing)*
- ☐ Snacks and drinks
- ☐ Sunshades/sunbeds
- ☑ Dogs allowed *(on the beach)*

Facilities: Three good toilet blocks include facilities for children and disabled visitors. Laundry facilities. Bar/snack bar. Shop. Takeaway. Swimming and paddling pools (heated all season). Gym. Bicycle hire. Games room. Playground. Activity and entertainment programme. Mobile homes and chalets for rent. Off site: Golf 100 m. Nearest beach 150 m. Fishing. Riding 200 m. Tennis. Quiberon. Carnac. Excursions to Belle Ile.

Open: 2 April - 2 October.

Directions: From Auray (RN 165) take the southbound D768 to Plouharnel and on to Quiberon. Upon arrival in Quiberon, follow signs to 'Thalassotherapie' and then to site. GPS: 47.47634, -3.110364

Charges guide

Per unit incl. 2 persons and electricity	€ 15,00 - € 40,00
extra person	€ 3,00 - € 7,00
child (3-6 yrs)	€ 2,50 - € 5,00
dog	€ 2,00

FRANCE – Bidart

Camping le Pavillon Royal

Avenue du Prince de Galles, F-64210 Bidart (Pyrénées-Atlantiques)
t: 05 59 23 00 54 e: info@pavillon-royal.com
alanrogers.com/FR64060 www.pavillon-royal.com

Accommodation: ☑ Pitch ☑ Mobile home/chalet ☐ Hotel/B&B ☐ Apartment

Le Pavillon Royal has an excellent situation on raised ground overlooking the sea, with good views along the coast to the south and to the north coast of Spain beyond. There is a large heated swimming pool and sunbathing area in the centre of the site. The camping area is divided up into 303 marked, level pitches, many of a good size. About 50 are reserved for tents and are only accessible on foot. The remainder are connected by asphalt roads. All have electricity and most are fully serviced. Much of the campsite is in full sun, although the area for tents is shaded. Beneath the site – and only a very short walk down – stretches a wide sandy beach where the Atlantic rollers provide ideal conditions for surfing. A central, marked-out section of the beach is supervised by lifeguards (from mid June). There is also a section with rocks and pools. Reservation in high season is advisable.

Special offers

Free use of the fitness suite and entry to the wellness centre. WiFi access.

You might like to know

The only campsite in the Basque country with direct access to the beach, where there is a surf school. The site also has a swimming pool heated by solar power.

- ☑ Beach on site
- ☑ Beach within 1 km
- ☑ Sandy beach
- ☐ Blue Flag quality
- ☑ Lifeguard *(high season)*
- ☐ Sun lounger and/or deckchair hire
- ☑ Watersports *(e.g. sailing or windsurfing)*
- ☑ Snacks and drinks
- ☑ Sunshades/sunbeds
- ☐ Dogs allowed *(on the beach)*

Facilities: Good quality toilet blocks with baby baths and two units for disabled visitors. Washing facilities (only two open at night). Washing machines, dryers. Motorcaravan services. Shop (including gas). Restaurant and takeaway (from 1/6). Bar (all season). Heated swimming and paddling pools. Playground. General room, TV room, games room, films. Fishing. Surf school. Fitness room. Wellness facilities (1/6-25/9). Dogs are not accepted. WiFi (charged). Off site: Golf 500 m. Bicycle hire 2 km. Riding 3 km. Sailing 5 km. New oceanographic centre at Biarritz.

Open: 14 May - 30 September.

Directions: From A63 exit 4, take the N10 south towards Bidart. At roundabout after the 'Intermarché' supermarket turn right (signed for Biarritz). After 600 m. turn left at site sign.
GPS: 43.45458, -1.57649

Charges guide

Per unit incl. 2 persons, electricity and water	€ 30,00 - € 51,00
tent incl. 1 or 2 persons	€ 24,00 - € 41,00
extra person (over 4 yrs)	€ 8,00 - € 11,00

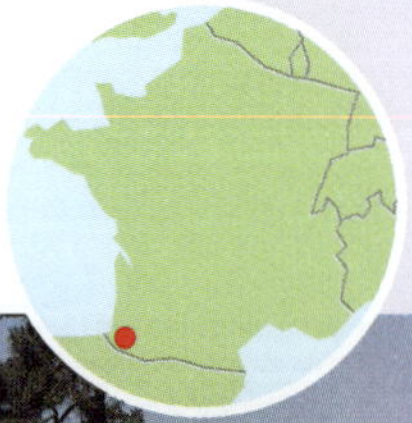

FRANCE – Argelès-sur-Mer

Camping le Littoral

Route du Littoral, F-66700 Argelès-sur-Mer (Pyrénées-Orientales)
t: 02 51 33 17 00 e: infos@camping-le-littoral.fr
alanrogers.com/FR66060 www.camp-atlantique.com

Accommodation: ☑ Pitch ☑ Mobile home/chalet ☐ Hotel/B&B ☐ Apartment

Sites with access to the beach are difficult to find and, even though le Littoral is not directly beside the beach, it is only 800 metres away by footpath. It offers much accommodation in mobile homes as well as 20 good sized, level touring pitches with shade and 6A electricity. An attractive pool area is open from May to September. Argelès is a very popular holiday resort with good sandy beaches. The border with Spain is only 30 km. The site is situated on the north side of Argelès between the coast road and the beach, so access is good, although there could be some road noise in high season. The site has been taken over by a new group, Camp'Atlantic and is looking smart with a new reception and tarmac roadways. However, there are now fewer touring pitches and the emphasis is on mobile homes with 127 to let and 105 privately owned. The site is well looked after and the pool area is particularly welcoming.

You might like to know

Don't miss the 'Déferlantes' music festival at Argelès-sur-Mer or the 'Fêtes de la Saint Vincent' at Collioure. The Abbey at Saint Martin du Canigou is definitely worth the climb.

- ☑ **Beach on site**
- ☐ **Beach within 1 km**
- ☑ **Sandy beach**
- ☑ **Blue Flag quality**
- ☐ **Lifeguard** *(high season)*
- ☐ **Sun lounger and/or deckchair hire**
- ☐ **Watersports** *(e.g. sailing or windsurfing)*
- ☐ **Snacks and drinks**
- ☐ **Sunshades/sunbeds**
- ☐ **Dogs allowed** *(on the beach)*

Facilities: Large modern toilet block, fully equipped and with some washbasins in cabins. Baby bath. Some facilities for disabled visitors. Washing machines. Shop. Bar, restaurant and takeaway (15/6-15/9). Heated swimming pool (May-Sept). Entertainment in high season. Play area. Bicycle hire. Internet. Path to beach. Communal barbecues only. Off site: Tourist train in high season. Aquatic park, adventure park, karting, riding and minigolf all within walking distance.

Open: 30 April - 24 September.

Directions: From A9 take exit 42 (Perpignan-Sud) and follow N114 for Argelès. At exit 10 follow directions for Taxo d'Avall then Plage Nord. Site is clearly signed off coast road in the St Cyprien direction. GPS: 42.580606, 3.032854

Charges guide

Per unit incl. 2 persons and electricity	€ 21,00 - € 44,00
extra person	€ 6,00 - € 9,00
child (0-10 yrs)	free - € 9,00
dog	€ 5,00

FRANCE – Canet-en-Roussillon

Yelloh! Village le Brasilia

B.P. 204, F-66141 Canet-en-Roussillon (Pyrénées-Orientales)
t: **04 68 80 23 82** e: **info@lebrasilia.fr**
alanrogers.com/FR66070 www.brasilia.fr

Accommodation: ☑ Pitch ☑ Mobile home/chalet ☐ Hotel/B&B ☐ Apartment

Situated across the yacht harbour from the upmarket resort of Canet-Plage, le Brasilia is an impressive, well managed family site directly beside the beach. It is pretty, neat and well kept with an amazingly wide range of facilities – indeed, it is camping at its best. There are 428 neatly hedged touring pitches, all with electricity (6-10A) and 315 with water and drainage. They vary in size from 80 to 120 sq.m. and some of the longer pitches are suitable for two families together. With a range of shade from pines and flowering shrubs, less on pitches near the beach, there are neat access roads (sometimes narrow for large units). There are also 161 pitches with mobile homes and chalets to rent (the new ones have their own gardens). The sandy beach here is busy, with a beach club (you can hire windsurfing boards) and a naturist section is on the beach to the west of the site. The village area of the site offers a range of shops, a busy restaurant and bar, entertainment (including a night club) and clubs for children.

You might like to know

This site has direct access to the 9 km. beach and nearby harbour of Canet-en-Rousillon, an up-market resort offering kitesurfing, windsurfing, diving and sailing lessons.

- ☑ **Beach on site**
- ☐ **Beach within 1 km**
- ☑ **Sandy beach**
- ☑ **Blue Flag quality**
- ☑ **Lifeguard** *(high season)*
- ☑ **Sun lounger and/or deckchair hire**
- ☑ **Watersports** *(e.g. sailing or windsurfing)*
- ☑ **Snacks and drinks**
- ☑ **Sunshades/sunbeds**
- ☐ **Dogs allowed** *(on the beach)*

Facilities: Ten modern sanitary blocks are very well equipped and maintained, with British style WCs (some Turkish) and washbasins in cabins. Good facilities for children and disabled visitors. Laundry room. Motorcaravan services. Shops. Gas supplies. Bars and restaurant. New pool complex (heated). Play areas. Sports field. Tennis. Sporting activities. Library, games and video room. Hairdresser. Internet café and WiFi. Daily entertainment. Bicycle hire. Fishing. ATM. Exchange facilities. Post office. Gas and electric barbecues are allowed. Off site: Boat launching and sailing 500 m. Riding 5 km. Golf 12 km.

Open: 21 April - 29 September.

Directions: From A9 exit 41 (Perpignan Centre, Rivesaltes) follow signs for Le Barcarès and Canet on D83 for 10 km. then for Canet (D81). At first Canet roundabout, turn fully back on yourself (Sainte-Marie) and watch for Brasilia sign almost immediately on right. GPS: 42.70467, 3.03483

Charges guide

Per unit incl. 2 persons and electricity (6A)	€ 23,00 - € 55,00
extra person	€ 6,00 - € 9,00
child (3-6 yrs)	free - € 8,50
dog (max. 2)	€ 4,00

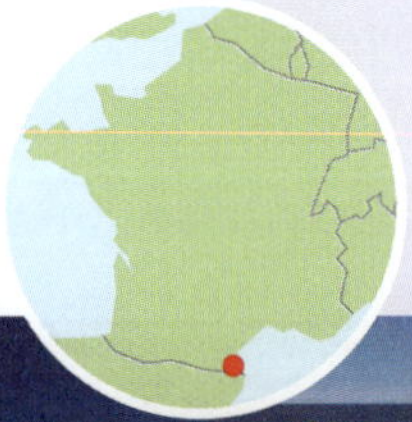

FRANCE – Argelès-sur-Mer

Camping la Sirène

Route de Taxo á la Mer, F-66702 Argelès-sur-Mer (Pyrénées-Orientales)
t: **04 68 81 04 61** e: **contact@camping-lasirene.fr**
alanrogers.com/FR66560 www.camping-lasirene.fr

Accommodation: ☑ Pitch ☑ Mobile home/chalet ☐ Hotel/B&B ☐ Apartment

From the moment you step into the hotel-like reception area you realise that this large site offers the holiday maker everything they could want in a well managed and convenient location close to Argelès-sur-Mer and the beaches. The 740 mobile homes and chalets vary in standard but all are less than five years old, very clean, comfortable and located on neat tidy pitches. There are also some touring pitches. In the summer there are 170 staff on duty to ensure your stay is as enjoyable as they can make it. All the shops and amenities are near reception making the accommodation areas quite peaceful and relaxing. There are many things to do and summer visitors have the option of using the free bus service to the beach where the site has its own club where you can even go windsurfing at no charge.

You might like to know

An area of the North beach is reserved for dogs.

- ☐ **Beach on site**
- ☑ **Beach within 1 km**
- ☑ **Sandy beach**
- ☑ **Blue Flag quality**
- ☑ **Lifeguard** *(high season)*
- ☑ **Sun lounger and/or deckchair hire**
- ☑ **Watersports** *(e.g. sailing or windsurfing)*
- ☑ **Snacks and drinks**
- ☑ **Sunshades/sunbeds**
- ☑ **Dogs allowed** *(on the beach)*

Facilities: Restaurant, bar and takeaway. Large shop (all season). Large aqua park, paddling pools, slides, jacuzzi. Games room. Multisports field, tennis, archery, minigolf, football. Theatre, evening entertainment, discos, show time spectacular. Riding. Bicycle hire. Off site: Resort of Argelès-sur-Mer with beaches, karting, 10-pin bowling, amusement park and the site's private Emeraude Beach Club, all 2 km. Interesting town of Collioure nearby. Fishing 4 km. Golf 7 km.

Open: 17 April - 26 September.

Directions: Leave A9 motorway, exit 42, take D114, towards Argelès. Leave D114, exit 10 and follow signs for Plage Nord. Site signed after first roundabout. Site on right 2 km. after last roundabout. GPS: 42.57093, 3.02906

Charges guide

Per unit incl. 1-3 persons and electricity	€ 26,00 - € 43,00
extra person	€ 6,00 - € 9,00
child (under 5 yrs)	€ 4,00 - € 6,00
dog	free

FRANCE – Argelès-sur-Mer

Camping le Bois du Valmarie

F-66702 Argelès-sur-Mer (Pyrénées-Orientales)
t: 04 68 81 09 92 e: contact@camping-lasirene.fr
alanrogers.com/FR66590 www.camping-lasirene.fr

Accommodation: ☐ Pitch ☑ Mobile home/chalet ☐ Hotel/B&B ☐ Apartment

Pitches here are exclusively for mobile home and chalet accommodation. Le Bois du Valmarie is a member of the same group of sites as la Sirène (FR66560). The site has 181 pitches, the majority of which are available for booking (none available for touring) and is located south of the port beside Racou beach. The site has a pleasant woodland location and a range of amenities including a large swimming pool complex with waterslides and a separate children's pool. The sea is just 50 m. from the site entrance with a sandy beach and within easy walking distance. The site has its own bar and a good restaurant but visitors are welcome at la Sirène to enjoy the entertainment and activities on offer. The site is popular with tour operators.

You might like to know

The site is on Racou beach with its 7 km. of golden sands, in an idyllic spot between the mountains and the sea. On an evening you can relax in the friendly atmosphere of its cosy bars and traditional restaurants.

- ☐ **Beach on site**
- ☑ **Beach within 1 km**
- ☐ **Sandy beach**
- ☑ **Blue Flag quality**
- ☑ **Lifeguard** *(high season)*
- ☐ **Sun lounger and/or deckchair hire**
- ☑ **Watersports** *(e.g. sailing or windsurfing)*
- ☑ **Snacks and drinks**
- ☑ **Sunshades/sunbeds**
- ☐ **Dogs allowed** *(on the beach)*

Facilities: Supermarket. Restaurant. Bar. Beach shop. Takeaway food. Swimming pool with waterslides and separate children's pool. Play area. Mobile homes for rent. Off site: Argelès town centre 3 km. Diving club. Blue Bear activity club. Emeraude Beach Club. Fishing 2 km. Riding 4 km. Golf 7 km.

Open: 7 April - 28 September.

Directions: Leave autoroute at Perpignan Sud exit and join the N114 southbound towards Argelès. Take exit 13 and follow signs to le Racou. Site is well signed from here.
GPS: 42.53784, 3.05445

Charges guide

Contact the site for details.

FRANCE – Bormes-les-Mimosas

Camp du Domaine

B.P. 207 La Favière, F-83230 Bormes-les-Mimosas (Var)
t: 04 94 71 03 12 e: mail@campdudomaine.com
alanrogers.com/FR83120 www.campdudomaine.com

Accommodation: ☑ Pitch ☑ Mobile home/chalet ☐ Hotel/B&B ☐ Apartment

Camp du Domaine, 3 km. south of Le Lavandou, is a large, attractive beachside site with 1,200 pitches set in 45 hectares of pinewood, although surprisingly it does not give the impression of being so big. The pitches are large (up to 200 sq.m) and most are reasonably level, 800 with 10A electricity. The most popular pitches are beside the beach, but the ones furthest away are generally larger and have more shade. Amongst the trees, many are more suitable for tents. The price for all the pitches is the same – smaller but near the beach or larger with shade. The beach is the attraction and everyone tries to get close. American motorhomes are not accepted. Despite its size, the site does not feel too busy, except perhaps around the supermarket. This is mainly because many pitches are hidden in the trees, the access roads are quite wide and it all covers quite a large area (some of the beach pitches are 600 m. from the entrance). Its popularity makes early reservation necessary over a long season (mid June to mid Sept).

Special offers

Hire a bungalow or mobile home for two weeks and get a 50% discount on the second week. Lowest prices are in May and June.

You might like to know

On the beach you will find all manner of watersports, a sailing school, a diving school and beach volleyball (in high season). From le Lavandou there are boat trips to the Iles d'Or (Port Cros and Porquerolles). Nearby is the Provençal village of Bormes les Mimosas.

- ☑ Beach on site
- ☐ Beach within 1 km
- ☑ Sandy beach
- ☐ Blue Flag quality
- ☑ Lifeguard *(high season)*
- ☑ Sun lounger and/or deckchair hire
- ☑ Watersports *(e.g. sailing or windsurfing)*
- ☑ Snacks and drinks
- ☑ Sunshades/sunbeds
- ☐ Dogs allowed *(on the beach)*

Facilities: Ten modern, well used but clean toilet blocks. Mostly Turkish WCs. Facilities for disabled visitors (but steep steps). Baby room. Washing machines. Fridge hire. Well stocked supermarket, bars, pizzeria. No swimming pool. Excellent play area. Boats, pedaloes for hire. Wide range of watersports. Children's club. Multisport courts. Games, competitions (July/Aug). Tennis. Barbecues are strictly forbidden. Dogs are not accepted 10/7-21/8. Off site: Bicycle hire 500 m. Riding and golf 15 km.

Open: 9 April - 5 November.

Directions: From Bormes-les-Mimosas, head east on D559 to Le Lavandou. At roundabout, turn off D559 towards the sea on road signed Favière. After 2 km. turn left at site signs.
GPS: 43.11779, 6.35176

Charges guide

Per unit incl. 2 persons and electricity	€ 28,50 - € 43,00
extra person	€ 6,00 - € 9,50
child (under 7 yrs)	€ 1,00 - € 4,80
dog (not 10/7-21/8)	free

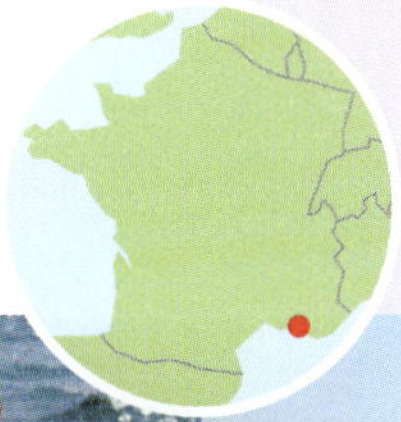

FRANCE – Le Lavandou

Camping Saint Pons

Avenue Maréchal Juin, F-83190 Le Lavandou (Var)
t: **04 94 71 03 93** e: **info@campingstpons.com**
alanrogers.com/FR83680 www.campingstpons.com

Accommodation: ☑ Pitch ☑ Mobile home/chalet ☐ Hotel/B&B ☐ Apartment

Camping Saint Pons enjoys an attractive setting within walking distance of the delightful family resort of Le Lavandou. This is a park-like site extending over two hectares, and with many flowering shrubs and bushes. There are 155 pitches here, well shaded and of a fair size. Most have electrical connections. A number of mobile homes are available for rent. There is no shop on site but there is a supermarket 500 m. away. The Littoral cycle track runs close to the site and provides an appealing way of exploring the coast and a number of pretty Provençal villages. Saint Pons is a relaxed site with little by way of on-site entertainment. There is a bar and restaurant next door. Le Lavandou is also one of the Riviera's more restrained resorts, named apparently after the river where local women came to do their washing because the water was so soft. The village boasts no fewer than 12 beaches, some wide and sandy, and others tiny, rocky coves. All can be reached by travelling on a small tourist train that runs along the coast.

You might like to know

There are no fewer than 12 beaches at Le Lavandou, including the Grande Plage, a fine sandy beach backed by palm trees.

- ☐ **Beach on site**
- ☑ **Beach within 1 km**
- ☑ **Sandy beach**
- ☑ **Blue Flag quality**
- ☑ **Lifeguard** *(high season)*
- ☑ **Sun lounger and/or deckchair hire**
- ☑ **Watersports** *(e.g. sailing or windsurfing)*
- ☑ **Snacks and drinks**
- ☑ **Sunshades/sunbeds**
- ☑ **Dogs allowed** *(on the beach)*

Facilities: Two clean sanitary blocks with controllable pushbutton showers. Wet room for disabled visitors. Laundry facilities. Children's playground. Boules. Tourist information. Mobile homes for rent. No pets (1/7-21/8). Off site: Le Lavandou 500 m. Nearest beach 800 m. Cycle tracks. Golf. Boat trips. Fishing.

Open: 1 May - 1 October.

Directions: From Hyères (A570) head east on D98 to Bormes-les-Mimosas and then south east on D559 to Le Lavandou, and then follow signs to the site. GPS: 43.136047, 6.354416

Charges guide

Per unit incl. 2 persons and electricity	€ 17,40 - € 28,20
extra person	€ 4,20 - € 6,00
child (under 7 yrs)	€ 3,00 - € 4,20
dog	€ 2,60 - € 3,80

FRANCE – Longeville-sur-Mer

Camping le Petit Rocher

1250 avenue de Docteur Mathevet, F-85560 Longeville-sur-Mer (Vendée)
t: 02 51 33 17 00 e: info@campinglepetitrocher.com
alanrogers.com/FR85000 www.camp-atlantique.com

Accommodation: ☑ Pitch ☑ Mobile home/chalet ☐ Hotel/B&B ☐ Apartment

A former municipal site, le Petit Rocher is now under the same management (M. Guignard) as another local campsite, les Brunelles. With its seaside location set in a pine forest, there is an air of peace and tranquillity. Although the area is undulating, the 150 good size touring pitches are flat and arranged in terraces over the wooded area. Electricity hook-ups are available (Euro style plugs) and there are adequate water points. A grassy play area for children is thoughtfully situated in a hollow, but has limited equipment. A fun pool was added in 2008. There are 28 unusual bungalows for rent which would not be out of place on a safari. Square in shape and constructed of wood they consist of a kitchen/living area and two bedrooms. Although some do not have sanitary facilities, there are ample facilities on the site.

You might like to know

The site is close to Plage du Rocher, one of three safe family beaches in the area. They are backed by pine forests, which have cycle tracks and are ideal for hiking and riding.

- ☐ Beach on site
- ☑ Beach within 1 km
- ☑ Sandy beach
- ☑ Blue Flag quality
- ☑ Lifeguard *(high season)*
- ☐ Sun lounger and/or deckchair hire
- ☑ Watersports *(e.g. sailing or windsurfing)*
- ☐ Snacks and drinks
- ☐ Sunshades/sunbeds
- ☑ Dogs allowed *(on the beach)*

Facilities: Three new, spacious sanitary blocks are clean and well maintained with showers, British style WCs. Facilities for people with disabilities. Washing machine and dryer. Bar, restaurant and takeaway (July/Aug). Tennis court. New heated outdoor pool (28/5-17/9). Max. 1 dog. Off site: Beach 200 m. Bars, restaurant, and small shops nearby. Riding and bicycle hire 2 km. Boat launching 11 km. Fishing 15 km. Golf 20 km.

Open: 28 May - 17 September.

Directions: From Longeville-sur-Mer follow signs for Le Rocher towards La Tranche-sur-Mer. Turn right at first roundabout, following campsite signs to site on right. GPS: 46.403767, -1.507183

Charges guide

Per unit incl. 2 persons and electricity	€ 16,00 - € 25,00
extra person	€ 3,00 - € 5,00
child (0-5 yrs)	free - € 3,00
dog	€ 5,00

FRANCE – Saint Jean-de-Monts

Camping Acapulco

Avenue des Epines, F-85160 Saint Jean-de-Monts (Vendée)
t: 02 51 54 33 87 e: info@sunmarina.com
alanrogers.com/FR85220 www.sunmarina.com

Accommodation: ☑ Pitch ☑ Mobile home/chalet ☐ Hotel/B&B ☐ Apartment

Ideal for family beach holidays, this large, friendly site is just 600 m. from the beach. Most of the 450 pitches here are taken by mobile homes; at present 40 are available for touring, although some of these are destined for more mobiles. The few existing touring pitches, which have electricity and water nearby, are of average size on grass and divided by hedges. There is an excellent pool complex with waterslides, a children's pool, an imaginative new 'balnéo' area and a sunbathing terrace. Adjacent to this is a spacious bar/restaurant. Acapulco is midway between the popular resort of Saint Jean-de-Monts and the more laid-back Saint Hilaire-de-Riez; as a result, the opportunities for shopping and eating out are many. The busy fishing port of Saint Gilles Croix-de-Vie, a little further south, has quayside bars and restaurants, pedestrianised streets and a thriving marina. Fashionable Les Sables d'Olonne, famous for its superb sandy beach and its great range of shops, bars and restaurants, is an easy drive away.

You might like to know

The Atlantic Toboggan water park is probably the best in the Vendée, and just 1,500 m. from the site.

- ☐ **Beach on site**
- ☑ **Beach within 1 km**
- ☑ **Sandy beach**
- ☑ **Blue Flag quality**
- ☑ **Lifeguard** *(high season)*
- ☑ **Sun lounger and/or deckchair hire**
- ☑ **Watersports** *(e.g. sailing or windsurfing)*
- ☑ **Snacks and drinks**
- ☐ **Sunshades/sunbeds**
- ☐ **Dogs allowed** *(on the beach)*

Facilities: Three sanitary blocks are clean and include washbasins in cabins and preset showers. Facilities for disabled visitors. Hot water to dishwashing and laundry sinks. Washing machines and dryers. Shop, takeaway and bar/restaurant. Heated, open-air pool complex. Play area. Tennis. Cycle hire. WiFi throughout (charged). Children's club and full programme of activities and entertainment plus excursions (July/Aug). Off site: Shopping centre 400 m. Sandy beach 600 m. Riding 2 km. Fishing, sailing and golf 6 km. St Jean-de-Monts 6 km. St Hilaire-de-Riez 8 km. St Gilles 10 km. Les Sables 40 km.

Open: 1 May - 11 September.

Directions: Saint Jean-de-Monts is 55 km. northwest of La Roche-sur-Yon. The site is off the D38 St Jean-de-Monts - Saint Gilles road at Orou't. At mini-roundabout by L'Oasis hotel/restaurant turn southwest signed Les Mouettes and campsite. Site is on left in 2 km. GPS: 46.7637, -2.009

Charges guide

Per unit incl. 3 persons and electricity	€ 25,00 - € 35,00
extra person	€ 9,00
child (under 5 yrs)	€ 6,00

FRANCE – Saint Jean-de-Monts

Camping la Forêt

190 chemin de la Rive, F-85160 Saint Jean-de-Monts (Vendée)
t: 02 51 58 84 63 e: camping-la-foret@wanadoo.fr
alanrogers.com/FR85360 www.hpa-laforet.com

Accommodation: ☑ Pitch ☑ Mobile home/chalet ☐ Hotel/B&B ☐ Apartment

Camping la Forêt is an attractive, well run site with a friendly family atmosphere, thanks to the hard working owners, M. and Mme. Jolivet. It provides just 63 pitches with 39 for touring units. They are of a reasonable size and surrounded by mature hedges; all have water and electricity, and some also have drainage. A variety of trees provide shade to every pitch. There are 13 mobile homes for rent and one tour operator on site (11 pitches), but their presence is not intrusive and the site has a quiet and relaxed atmosphere. La Forêt is an ideal choice for couples or families with young children wanting to be close to the sea but not looking for on-site entertainment and activities. The owners run their site on sound ecological principles and have invested heavily in measures to save energy and help the environment. The beach is just a 400 m. walk away, while the lively resort of Saint Jean-de-Monts with a wide choice of shops, bars and restaurants plus daily markets is just 6 km. away.

You might like to know

The nearby fine sandy beach is away from the public gaze and popular with nature lovers. A variety of sporting events take place on Grande Plage at Saint Jean-de-Monts including triathlon, sand-sculpture, beach volleyball, sand yachting and riding.

- ☐ **Beach on site**
- ☑ **Beach within 1 km**
- ☑ **Sandy beach**
- ☑ **Blue Flag quality**
- ☐ **Lifeguard** *(high season)*
- ☐ **Sun lounger and/or deckchair hire**
- ☑ **Watersports** *(e.g. sailing or windsurfing)*
- ☑ **Snacks and drinks**
- ☑ **Sunshades/sunbeds**
- ☑ **Dogs allowed** *(on the beach)*

Facilities: The central toilet block has hot showers and washbasins in cubicles. Laundry and dishwashing facilities. Baby bath. Facilities for disabled visitors. Motorcaravan waste tanks emptied on request. Basic provisions sold in reception, including fresh bread. Takeaway (15/5-15/9). Small heated swimming pool (15/5-15/9). Small games room with TV. WiFi (charged). Play area. Bicycle hire. Only gas and electric barbecues allowed. Not suitable for American motorhomes. Off site: Beach 400 m. Sailing 1 km. Golf 2 km. Riding 3 km. Shop, bar and restaurant within 2 km. and in St Jean-de-Monts 6 km. Noirmoutier 10 km. Cycling paths through the forest.

Open: 1 May - 28 September.

Directions: The site is 6 km. north of St Jean-de-Monts just off the D38 towards Notre Dame-de-Monts. At southern end of Notre Dame, turn west at sign for site and Plage de Pont d'Yeu. Bear left and site is on left in about 200 m.
GPS: 46.80807, -2.11384

Charges guide

Per unit incl. 2 persons and electricity	€ 18,90 - € 31,90
extra person	€ 3,50 - € 5,00
child (under 7 yrs)	€ 3,50 - € 3,90

FRANCE – Longeville-sur-Mer

Camping les Brunelles

Le Bouil, F-85560 Longeville-sur-Mer (Vendée)
t: **02 51 33 17 00** e: **camping@les-brunelles.com**
alanrogers.com/FR85440 www.camp-atlantique.com

Accommodation: ☑ Pitch ☑ Mobile home/chalet ☐ Hotel/B&B ☐ Apartment

This is a well managed site with a wide range of facilities and a varied programme of high season entertainment for all the family. A busy site in high season, there are plenty of activities to keep children happy and occupied. In 2007 les Brunelles was combined with an adjacent campsite to provide 600 pitches of which 200 are for touring units; all have electricity (10A) and 20 of the new touring pitches also have water and a drain. All are in excess of 100 sq.m. to allow easier access for larger units. On the original les Brunelles site, the touring pitches are all level on sandy grass and separated by hedges, away from most of the mobile homes. A large aquapark provides a swimming pool of 1,000 sq.m. with indoor and outdoor pools, slides, a sauna, steam room, jacuzzi, and a fitness centre. A good, supervised, sandy beach is 900 m. away.

You might like to know

There are three sandy beaches within easy reach, as well as a number of surfing and sailing schools.

- ☐ **Beach on site**
- ☑ **Beach within 1 km**
- ☑ **Sandy beach**
- ☐ **Blue Flag quality**
- ☐ **Lifeguard** *(high season)*
- ☐ **Sun lounger and/or deckchair hire**
- ☑ **Watersports** *(e.g. sailing or windsurfing)*
- ☐ **Snacks and drinks**
- ☐ **Sunshades/sunbeds**
- ☐ **Dogs allowed** *(on the beach)*

Facilities: Four well maintained and modernised toilet blocks have British and Turkish style toilets and washbasins, both open style and in cabins. Laundry facilities. Shop, takeaway and large modern, airy bar (all season). Covered pool with jacuzzi (all season). Outdoor pool with slides and paddling pools (21/5-24/9). Tennis. Bicycle hire. Max. 1 dog. Off site: Riding 3 km. Good, supervised, sandy beach 900 m. St Vincent-sur-Jard 2 km. Golf 20 km.

Open: 2 April - 24 September.

Directions: From D21 (Talmont-Longeville), between St Vincent and Longeville, site signed south from main road towards coast. Turn left in Le Bouil (site is signed). Site is 800 m. on left.
GPS: 46.41330, -1.52313

Charges guide

Per unit incl. 2 persons and electricity	€ 21,00 - € 35,00
incl. water and drain	€ 25,00 - € 40,00
extra person	€ 5,00 - € 9,00
child (under 5 yrs)	free - € 6,00
dog	€ 5,00

UNITED KINGDOM – Newquay

Trevornick Holiday Park

Holywell Bay, Newquay TR8 5PW (Cornwall)
t: 01637 830531 e: bookings@trevornick.co.uk
alanrogers.com/UK0220 www.trevornick.co.uk

Accommodation: ☑ Pitch ☐ Mobile home/chalet ☐ Hotel/B&B ☐ Apartment

Trevornick, once a working farm, is a modern, busy and well run family touring park providing a very wide range of amenities close to one of Cornwall's finest beaches. A modern reception with welcoming staff sets the tone for your holiday. The park has grown to provide caravanners and campers (no holiday caravans but 56 very well equipped Eurotents) with some 550 large grass pitches (350 with 10A electricity and 55 fully serviced with electricity, water, drainage and TV connection with DVD channel) on five level fields and two terraced areas. There are few trees but some good views. Providing 'all singing, all dancing' facilities for fun packed family holidays, the farm buildings now provide the setting for the Farm Club. Recently refurbished, it provides much entertainment, from bingo and quizzes to shows, discos and cabaret. The Stables Grill also opens for breakfast and the Hungry Horse provides takeaway food.

You might like to know

Surfing is one of the most popular sports in Cornwall and Trevornick Holiday Park is only a short walk away from the beautiful Holywell Bay beach, which attracts surfers from far and wide.

- ☐ **Beach on site**
- ☑ **Beach within 1 km**
- ☑ **Sandy beach**
- ☐ **Blue Flag quality**
- ☐ **Lifeguard** *(high season)*
- ☐ **Sun lounger and/or deckchair hire**
- ☑ **Watersports** *(e.g. sailing or windsurfing)*
- ☑ **Snacks and drinks**
- ☐ **Sunshades/sunbeds**
- ☐ **Dogs allowed** *(on the beach)*

Facilities: Five modern toilet blocks provide showers, two family bathrooms, baby bath, laundry facilities and provision for disabled visitors. Well stocked supermarket with bread made on site (from late May). Hire Shop. Bars (with TV), restaurant, café and takeaway. Entertainment. Pool complex with heated outdoor pool, paddling pool, sunbathing decks, solarium, sauna and massage chair. Health and beauty salon. Super Fort Knox style adventure playground, crazy golf, Kiddies Club. Amusement arcade and bowling alley. Teenagers' room. 18-hole pitch and putt with golf pro shop. Bicycle hire. Coarse fishing in three lakes. Dogs are accepted in two fields only. Only limited facilities open at Easter and from 8 Sept. Off site: Riding 2 miles. Bicycle hire and boat launching 4 miles.

Open: Easter; mid May - mid September.

Directions: From A3075 approach to Newquay - Perranporth road, turn towards Cubert and Holywell Bay. Continue through Cubert to park on the right. GPS: 50.384983, -5.128933

Charges guide

Per unit incl. 2 persons and electricity	£ 16,15 - £ 26,05
extra person	£ 5,45 - £ 10,20
child (3-14 yrs)	£ 1,45 - £ 7,20

UNITED KINGDOM – Woolacombe

Woolacombe Sands Holiday Park

Beach Road, Woolacombe EX34 7AF (Devon)
t: 01271 870569 e: lifesabeach@woolacombe-sands.co.uk
alanrogers.com/UK0735 www.woolacombe-sands.co.uk

Accommodation: ☑ Pitch ☑ Mobile home/chalet ☐ Hotel/B&B ☐ Apartment

With sea views and within walking distance of Woolacombe's lovely sandy beach, this family park has been terraced out of the valley side as you drop down into the village. Apart from its smart entrance, it has been left natural. The pond and stream at the bottom are almost hidden with gated access to the National Trust fields across the valley. The 200 terraced level grass pitches, all with 16A electricity, are accessed by gravel roads with some good up-and-down walking needed to the toilet blocks (may pose a problem for visitors with disabilities). Some 50 mobile homes and 14 bungalows are in the more central area, and tents tend to be placed on the bottom terraces. The park boasts both indoor and outdoor pools (accessed by code) with a full time attendant. Upstairs from the indoor pool is a very pleasant conservatory seating area with great views and an outside seating area adjacent to it. Evenings see Woolly Bear emerge from his shack to entertain children, with adult family entertainment later.

You might like to know

Situated on the North Devon coast two miles west of Bideford, The BIG Sheep (a key member of Devon's Top Attractions) is an all-weather family attraction devoted to sheep and offering a wide range of indoor and outdoor activities.

- ☐ **Beach on site**
- ☑ **Beach within 1 km**
- ☑ **Sandy beach**
- ☑ **Blue Flag quality**
- ☑ **Lifeguard** *(high season)*
- ☐ **Sun lounger and/or deckchair hire**
- ☑ **Watersports** *(e.g. sailing or windsurfing)*
- ☑ **Snacks and drinks**
- ☐ **Sunshades/sunbeds**
- ☑ **Dogs allowed** *(on the beach)*

Facilities: Four basic toilet blocks with good hot water are spread amongst the terraces. The newer shower block has separate toilets opposite. Shop. Self-service food bar providing good value meals and breakfast (main season and B.Hs). Two bars and full entertainment programme. Heated indoor and outdoor pools both with paddling pool areas. Fenced play area on bark with plenty of equipment. Ball area with nets. Crazy golf. Kingpin bowling. Off site: Riding next door. Golf, bicycle hire and freshwater fishing 0.5 miles. Beach 15 minutes walk or 0.5 miles.

Open: 1 April - 30 October.

Directions: Follow the A361 from Barnstaple through Braunton towards Ilfracombe. At the Mullacott Cross roundabout turn left for on the B3343 for Woolacombe. Site clearly signed on left as you go down the hill into the village. GPS: 51.17145, -4.191833

Charges guide

Per person (incl. electricity)	£ 5,00 - £ 15,00
child (4-15 yrs)	£ 2,50 - £ 7,50
dog	£ 5,00

UNITED KINGDOM – Paignton

Beverley Park

Goodrington Road, Paignton TQ4 7JE (Devon)
t: **01803 661978** e: **info@beverley-holidays.co.uk**
alanrogers.com/UK0870 www.beverley-holidays.co.uk

Accommodation: ☑ Pitch ☑ Mobile home/chalet ☐ Hotel/B&B ☐ Apartment

Beverley Park is an amazing holiday centre catering for every need. It has been developed and run by the Jeavons family for over 50 years to very high standards. It is popular, busy and attractively landscaped with marvellous views over Torbay. The pools, a large dance hall, bars and entertainment, are all run in an efficient and orderly manner. The park has 190 caravan holiday homes and 23 lodges, mainly around the central complex. There are 179 touring pitches in the lower areas of the park, all reasonably sheltered, some with views across the bay and some on slightly sloping ground. All pitches can take awnings and 87 have 16A electricity (15 m. cable), 38 have hardstanding and 42 are fully serviced. Tents are accepted and a limited number of tent pitches have electrical connections. The park is open all year and reservations are essential for caravans in high season. Entertainment is organised at Easter and from early May in the Starlight Cabaret bar. A member of the Best of British Group.

You might like to know

No visit to Devon would be complete without a day at Dartmoor's famous Becky Falls, where there really is something for everyone to enjoy. Set within a spectacular ancient valley, the Falls have been attracting visitors for over 100 years.

- ☐ **Beach on site**
- ☑ **Beach within 1 km**
- ☑ **Sandy beach**
- ☑ **Blue Flag quality**
- ☐ **Lifeguard** *(high season)*
- ☐ **Sun lounger and/or deckchair hire**
- ☑ **Watersports** *(e.g. sailing or windsurfing)*
- ☐ **Snacks and drinks**
- ☐ **Sunshades/sunbeds**
- ☐ **Dogs allowed** *(on the beach)*

Facilities: Good toilet blocks adjacent to the pitches, well maintained and heated, include roomy showers, some with washbasins en-suite. Baths on payment. Unit for disabled visitors. Facilities for babies. Laundry. Gas supplies. Motorcaravan service point. Large general shop (30/3-26/10). Restaurant, bars and takeaway (all 13/3-15/4, 4/5-28/9, and 20/10-26/10). Heated swimming pools (outdoor 22/5-4/9, indoor all year). Fitness centre. Tennis. Crazy golf. Playground. Nature trail. Amusement centre with pool, table tennis and amusement machines. Soft play area. WiFi throughout. Dogs are not accepted. Off site: Regular minibus service to Paignton, bus services outside the park. Fishing, bicycle hire, riding and golf within 2 miles.

Open: All year.

Directions: Park is south of Paignton in Goodrington Road between A379 coast road and B3203 ring road and is well signed on both. GPS: 50.413533, -3.568667

Charges guide

Per unit incl. 2 persons and electricity	£ 15,20 - £ 38,50
tent pitch incl. 2 persons	£ 13,00 - £ 29,30
extra person	£ 4,70
child	£ 3,50

UNITED KINGDOM – Burnham-on-Sea

Northam Farm Touring Park

Brean Sands, Burnham-on-Sea TA8 2SE (Somerset)
t: **01278 751244** e: **enquiries@northamfarm.co.uk**
alanrogers.com/UK1570 www.northamfarm.co.uk

Accommodation: ☑ Pitch ☑ Mobile home/chalet ☐ Hotel/B&B ☐ Apartment

Brean has been a popular holiday destination for decades and many large campsites have evolved. Northam Farm, owned by the Scott family, is one of them. It is a family park with good facilities and ongoing improvements. Of the 750 pitches, 300 are for seasonal units and these are separated from the four touring fields. Pitches are well established and many have block paved hardstanding. There are two play areas for youngsters, a playing field, bicycle track and football pitch for teenagers, and fishing on the lake for adults. The owners and staff are always available to help visitors enjoy their stay. A monthly newsletter is published giving details of 'what's on' both on and off site. About 500 yards down the road is The Seagull, which is also owned by Northam Farm. Here you'll find an excellent restaurant, bar and nightly live entertainment, even during the low season. Just down the road is Brean Leisure Park with its swimming complex, funfair, golf and much more.

You might like to know

Northam Farm is ideally situated for exploring Somerset, a county of real diversity. Unmissable attractions include Cheddar caves and gorge, Wookey Hole, Wells cathedral, Glastonbury Tor plus traditional cider farms, museums and castles.

- ☐ **Beach on site**
- ☑ **Beach within 1 km**
- ☑ **Sandy beach**
- ☐ **Blue Flag quality**
- ☐ **Lifeguard** *(high season)*
- ☐ **Sun lounger and/or deckchair hire**
- ☐ **Watersports** *(e.g. sailing or windsurfing)*
- ☐ **Snacks and drinks**
- ☐ **Sunshades/sunbeds**
- ☑ **Dogs allowed** *(on the beach)*

Facilities: Three good toilet blocks are well maintained with ample toilets, washbasins and spacious showers (50p). Bathrooms (£1 charge). Baby room. Rooms for visitors with disabilities (radar key access). Laundry. Motorcaravan service point. Dog shower and two exercise areas. Licensed shop well stocked with food, holiday gear and accessories. Snack bar with takeaway. Free entry to live entertainment at The Seagull. Two play areas. Playing field. Fishing lake. Caravan workshop for repairs and servicing. Caravan storage. Dogs are not accepted in some of the fields. A bus stops at the park entrance. Off site: Beach 200 m. across road. Golf, bicycle hire and riding 0.5 miles. Burnham-on-Sea 4 miles. Weston-Super-Mare 8 miles.

Open: March - October.

Directions: From M5 junction 22 follow signs to Burnham-on-Sea, Berrow and then Brean. Continue through Brean and Northam Farm is on the right, half a mile past Brean Leisure Park. GPS: 51.2949, -3.010167

Charges guide

Per unit incl. 2 persons and electricity	£ 10,50 - £ 25,25
extra person	£ 2,00 - £ 2,50
child (0-15 yrs)	£ 1,00

UNITED KINGDOM – Milford-on-Sea

Lytton Lawn Touring Park

Lymore Lane, Milford-on-Sea SO41 0TX (Hampshire)
t: 01590 648331 e: holidays@shorefield.co.uk
alanrogers.com/UK2280 www.shorefield.co.uk

Accommodation: ☑ Pitch ☐ Mobile home/chalet ☐ Hotel/B&B ☐ Apartment

Lytton Lawn is the touring arm of Shorefield Country Park, a nearby holiday home park and leisure centre. Set in eight acres, it provides 135 marked pitches. These include 53 premier pitches (hardstanding, 16A electricity, pitch light, water and waste water outlet) in a grassy, hedged area – this section with its heated toilet block is open for a longer season. The rest of the pitches, all with electricity, are in the adjoining, but separate, gently sloping field, edged with mature trees and hedges and with a further toilet block. The larger reception and well stocked shop make this a good, comfortable, self-sufficient site. Visitors to Lytton Lawn are entitled to use the comprehensive leisure facilities at Shorefield itself (2.5 miles away). These include a very attractive indoor pool, solarium, sauna and spa, fitness classes and treatments, all-weather tennis courts, outdoor pools, restaurant facilities including a bistro (Easter-November), and entertainment and activity programmes.

Special offers

Free use of facilities at our main park 2.5 miles away. Please see website for special offers.

You might like to know

The New Forest is just two miles inland, and Bournemouth beach is only 12 miles away.

- ☐ **Beach on site**
- ☑ **Beach within 1 km**
- ☐ **Sandy beach**
- ☐ **Blue Flag quality**
- ☐ **Lifeguard** *(high season)*
- ☐ **Sun lounger and/or deckchair hire**
- ☑ **Watersports** *(e.g. sailing or windsurfing)*
- ☑ **Snacks and drinks**
- ☐ **Sunshades/sunbeds**
- ☑ **Dogs allowed** *(on the beach)*

Facilities: Two modern toilet blocks are well equipped. Washing machine and dryer. Baby changing. Facilities for disabled visitors (Radar key). Motorcaravan service point. Shop (February - December). Small fenced play area and hedged field with goal posts. Tents for rent. Off site: Village pub 10 minutes walk. Sailing, windsurfing and boat launching facilities 1.5 miles. Golf, riding, coarse fishing within 3 miles. The New Forest, Isle of Wight, Bournemouth, Southampton and the beach at Milford on Sea are nearby.

Open: All year excl. 3 January - 4 February.

Directions: From M27 follow signs for Lyndhurst and Lymington on A337. Continue towards New Milton and Lytton Lawn is signed at Everton; Shorefield is signed at Downton.
GPS: 50.73497, -1.61803

Charges guide

Per unit incl. 6 persons and electricity	£ 12,00 - £ 36,00
premier pitch incl. water, drainage and TV connection	£ 14,50 - £ 39,50
dog	£ 1,50 - £ 3,00

UNITED KINGDOM – Cromer

Woodhill Park

Cromer Road, East Runton, Cromer NR27 9PX (Norfolk)
t: **01263 512242** e: **info@woodhill-park.com**
alanrogers.com/UK3500 www.woodhill-park.com

Accommodation: ☑ Pitch ☑ Mobile home/chalet ☐ Hotel/B&B ☐ Apartment

Woodhill is a seaside site with good views and a traditional atmosphere. It is situated on the clifftop, in a large, gently sloping, open grassy field, with 300 marked touring pitches. Of these, 210 have electricity (16A), seven are fully serviced and many have wonderful views over the surrounding coastline and countryside. A small number of holiday homes are available with magnificent sea views. Although the site is fenced, there is access to the clifftop path which takes you to the beach. Locally, it is possible to take a boat trip to see the seals off Blakeney Point. Nearby attractions include the Shire Horse Centre at West Runton and the North Norfolk Steam Railway. Green technology plays a major role with solar panels added to one of the block roofs to heat the water. Access to nearby towns and resorts is available using the local bus stop outside the entrance, or by the tourist railway.

Special offers

Visit www.woodhill-park.com for the latest available offers.

You might like to know

The site overlooks a long sandy beach with rock pools – ideal for crabbing. There are several coastal walks to enjoy and nearby trips to see the seals at Blakeney Point.

- ☐ **Beach on site**
- ☑ **Beach within 1 km**
- ☑ **Sandy beach**
- ☑ **Blue Flag quality**
- ☑ **Lifeguard** *(high season)*
- ☐ **Sun lounger and/or deckchair hire**
- ☑ **Watersports** *(e.g. sailing or windsurfing)*
- ☑ **Snacks and drinks**
- ☐ **Sunshades/sunbeds**
- ☐ **Dogs allowed** *(on the beach)*

Facilities: Two modern toilet blocks with all necessary facilities including two family rooms with bath, showers, basin and WC, and four rooms with shower, basin and WC. Washing machine and dryer. Well stocked shop (19/3-31/10). Good, large adventure playground and plenty of space for ball games. Crazy golf. Giant chess and golf course adjacent to the site. Off site: Beach 0.5 miles. Fishing and shop 1 mile. Bicycle hire, golf and riding 2 miles. Bird Reserve at Cley. National Trust properties. North Norfolk Tourist Railway. Boat trips.

Open: 19 March - 31 October.

Directions: Site is beside the A149 coast road between East and West Runton.
GPS: 52.93742, 1.26250

Charges guide

Per unit incl. 2 persons and electricity	£ 15,65 - £ 18,95
extra person	£ 2,60
child (4-16 yrs)	£ 1,05
dog	£ 2,15 - £ 3,75

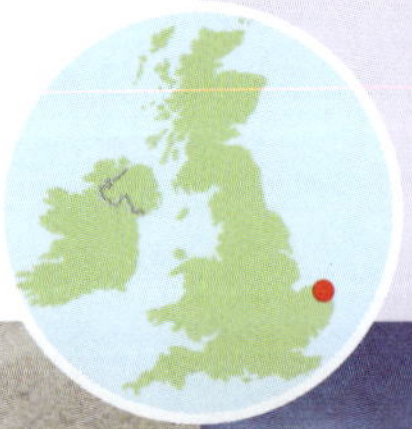

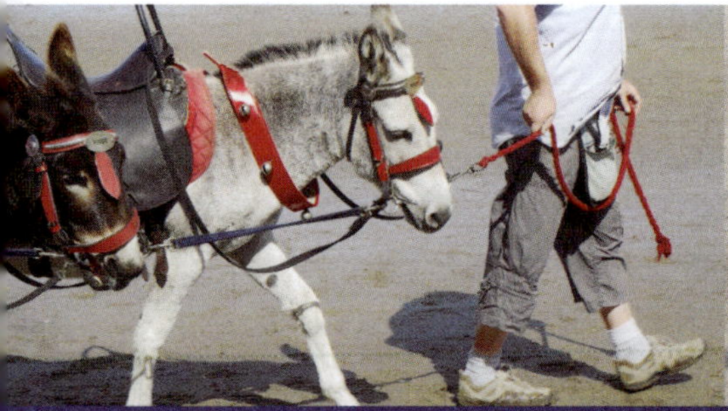

UNITED KINGDOM – Barmouth

Hendre Mynach Touring Park

Llanaber, Barmouth LL42 1YR (Gwynedd)
t: **01341 280262** e: **mynach@lineone.net**
alanrogers.com/UK6370 www.hendremynach.co.uk

Accommodation: ☑Pitch ☑Mobile home/chalet ☐Hotel/B&B ☐ Apartment

A neat and tidy family park, colourful flowers and top rate facilities make an instant impression on arrival down the steep entrance to this park (help is available to get out if you are worried). Of the 240 pitches, 60 are for touring guests and are allocated in various areas, with substantial tenting areas identified. All 60 touring pitches are fully serviced with electricity, water taps and waste water. The beach is only 100 yards away but is separated from the park by a railway line. It can be crossed by pedestrian operated gates, which could be a worry for those with young children. The quaint old seaside and fishing town of Barmouth is about a 30 minute walk along the prom. Here you will find 'everything'. Reception will provide leaflets with maps of local walks. Snowdonia National Park and mountain railway, the famous Ffestiniog railway, and castles and lakes everywhere provide plenty to see and do – this is a classic park in a classic area.

You might like to know

Aberdovey was once an important shipbuilding town, but is now a popular resort on the River Dyfi with a fine Blue Flag beach.

- ☐ **Beach on site**
- ☑ **Beach within 1 km**
- ☑ **Sandy beach**
- ☑ **Blue Flag quality**
- ☐ **Lifeguard** *(high season)*
- ☐ **Sun lounger and/or deckchair hire**
- ☑ **Watersports** *(e.g. sailing or windsurfing)*
- ☐ **Snacks and drinks**
- ☐ **Sunshades/sunbeds**
- ☐ **Dogs allowed** *(on the beach)*

Facilities: Two toilet blocks, one modern and one traditional, both offer excellent facilities including spacious showers (free) and washbasins in cubicles. An extension to the traditional block has added a good unit for disabled visitors with ramp access. Motorcaravan service point. Well stocked shop incorporating a snack bar and takeaway (Easter-1/11). WiFi. Off site: Beach 100 m. Fishing, boat launching and bicycle hire within 0.5 miles. Riding 5 miles. Golf 9 miles.

Open: All year excl. 10 January - 28 February.

Directions: Park is off the A496 road north of Barmouth in village of Llanaber with entrance down a steep drive. GPS: 52.73300, -4.06618

Charges guide

Per unit incl. 2 persons and electricity	£ 17,00 - £ 29,00
extra person	£ 4,00
child (2-14 yrs)	£ 2,00
first dog free, extra dog	£ 1,00

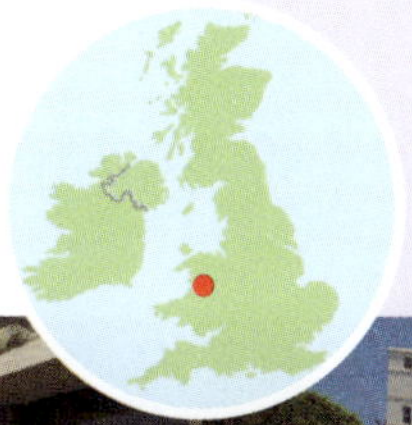

UNITED KINGDOM – Scourie

Scourie Caravan & Camping Park

Harbour Road, Scourie IV27 4TG (Highland)
t: **01971 502060**
alanrogers.com/UK7730

Accommodation: ☑ Pitch ☐ Mobile home/chalet ☐ Hotel/B&B ☐ Apartment

Mr Mackenzie has carefully nurtured this park over many years, developing a number of firm terraces with 60 pitches which gives it an attractive layout – there is nothing regimented here. Perched on the edge of the bay in an elevated position, practically everyone has a view of the sea and a short walk along the shore footpath leads to a small sandy beach. The park has tarmac and gravel access roads, with well drained grass and hardstanding pitches, some with 10A electric hook-ups. A few are on an area which is unfenced from the rocks (young children would need to be supervised here). Reception, alongside the modern toilet block, contains a wealth of tourist information and maps. There are very good facilities for disabled visitors on the park and at the restaurant, although the ramps leading to them are a little steep. Mr Mackenzie claims that this is the only caravan park in the world where, depending on the season, you can see palm trees, Highland cattle and Great Northern divers from your pitch.

You might like to know

The small sandy beach is a short walk from the site. It has crystal-clear water and is great for swimming and fishing from the rocks. There is also a bird hide.

- ☐ **Beach on site**
- ☑ **Beach within 1 km**
- ☑ **Sandy beach**
- ☐ **Blue Flag quality**
- ☐ **Lifeguard** *(high season)*
- ☐ **Sun lounger and/or deckchair hire**
- ☐ **Watersports** *(e.g. sailing or windsurfing)*
- ☐ **Snacks and drinks**
- ☐ **Sunshades/sunbeds**
- ☐ **Dogs allowed** *(on the beach)*

Facilities: The toilet facilities can be heated. Showers have no divider or seat. Laundry. Motorcaravan service point. The Anchorage restaurant at the entrance to the park (used as reception at quiet times) serves meals at reasonable prices, cooked to order (1/4-30/9). Boat launching. Fishing permits can be arranged. Off site: Village with shop and post office, gas is available from the petrol station and mobile banks visit regularly.

Open: Easter/1 April - 30 September, but phone first to check.

Directions: Park is by Scourie village on A894 road in northwest Sutherland.
GPS: 58.351417, -5.156767

Charges guide

Per unit incl. 2 persons	£ 12,00 - £ 16,00
electricity	£ 2,00
extra person	£ 2,50
child (3-16 yrs)	£ 1,50

No credit cards.

IRELAND – Rosslare Harbour

St Margaret's Beach Caravan Park

Lady's Island, Rosslare Harbour (Co. Wexford)
t: 053 913 1169 e: info@campingstmargarets.ie
alanrogers.com/IR9170 www.campingstmargarets.ie/

Accommodation: ☑ Pitch ☑ Mobile home/chalet ☐ Hotel/B&B ☐ Apartment

'This park is loved', was how a Swedish visitor described this environmentally-friendly, family-run caravan and camping park, the first the visitor meets near the Rosslare ferry port. Landscaping with flowering containers and maze-like sheltered camping areas and a pretty sanitary block all demonstrate the Traynor family's attention to detail. Most pitches give shelter from the fresh sea breeze and ferries can be seen crossing the Irish sea. Just metres away, the safe, sandy beach (part of the Wexford coastal path) curves around in a horseshoe shape ending in a small pier and slipway. Tourist information on the area is provided in the well stocked shop. The immediate area boasts of thatched roof cottages and cottage gardens. The park is an ideal base from which to explore the sunny southeast or as a stopover while touring Ireland, or for departure. Local lakes and the Saltee Islands, various locations of ornithological interest, deep sea and shore fishing, and award-winning pubs and restaurants provide something for everyone.

You might like to know

The safe sandy beach is on the Wexford Coastal path. Lady's Island and lake, the site of an ancient monastry, can be found along the coast. Also recommended are Kilmore Quay and Marina and Curracloe beach.

- ☐ Beach on site
- ☑ Beach within 1 km
- ☑ Sandy beach
- ☐ Blue Flag quality
- ☐ Lifeguard *(high season)*
- ☐ Sun lounger and/or deckchair hire
- ☑ Watersports *(e.g. sailing or windsurfing)*
- ☐ Snacks and drinks
- ☐ Sunshades/sunbeds
- ☐ Dogs allowed *(on the beach)*

Facilities: The toilet block is spotless. Laundry room. Campers' kitchen including toaster, microwave and TV. Shop (June-Aug). Fresh milk and bread daily. Mobile homes for rent. Sun/TV room. WiFi (charged). Off site: Walking, beach and fishing. Boat slipway 2.5 km. Pitch and putt 2 km. Riding 6 km. Pubs and restaurants. The JFK Arboretum, Johnstown Castle and Gardens, the Irish National Heritage Park, Kilmore Quay and Marina, and Curracloe beach (featured in the film Saving Private Ryan).

Open: Mid March - 31 October.

Directions: From the N25 south of Wexford town, outside village of Tagoat, follow signs for Lady's Island and Carne. After 3 km. pass Butler's Bar and take next left and continue for 2.5 km. Site is well signed.
GPS: 52.206433, -6.356417

Charges guide

Per unit incl. 2 persons and electricity	€ 22,00 - € 24,00
extra person	€ 2,50
child (2-16 yrs)	€ 1,50

IRELAND – Tuosist

Beara Camping The Peacock

Coornagillagh, Tuosist (Co. Kerry)
t: **064 668 4287** e: **bearacamping@eircom.net**
alanrogers.com/IR9580 www.bearacamping.com

Accommodation: ☑ Pitch ☑ Mobile home/chalet ☑ Hotel/B&B ☐ Apartment

Five minutes from Kenmare Bay, The Peacock is a unique location for campers who appreciate the natural world, where disturbance to nature is kept to a minimum. This five-acre site offers simple, clean and imaginative camping facilities. Located on the Ring of Beara, bordering the counties of Cork and Kerry, visitors will be treated with hospitality by a Dutch couple, Bert and Klaske van Bavel, almost more Irish than the Irish, who have made Ireland their home and run the site with their family. The variety of accommodation at Beara Camping includes a hostel, caravan holiday homes, secluded hardstanding pitches with electricity and level grass areas for tenting. In addition, there are cabins sleeping two or four people and hiker huts sleeping two, ideal to avoid a damp night or to dry out. Bert and Klaske love to share with visitors the unspoiled natural terrain, its wildlife, the sheltered community campfire and advice on the walking and hiking routes in the area.

You might like to know

This site is situated on the beautiful Beara Peninsula, only 5 km. from Kenmare Bay. Here you will find marine and wildlife including seals.

- ☐ **Beach on site**
- ☑ **Beach within 1 km**
- ☐ **Sandy beach**
- ☐ **Blue Flag quality**
- ☐ **Lifeguard** *(high season)*
- ☐ **Sun lounger and/or deckchair hire**
- ☐ **Watersports** *(e.g. sailing or windsurfing)*
- ☐ **Snacks and drinks**
- ☐ **Sunshades/sunbeds**
- ☐ **Dogs allowed** *(on the beach)*

Facilities: Three small blocks, plus facilities at the restaurant provide toilets, washbasins and free hot showers. Laundry service for a small fee. Campers' kitchens and sheltered eating area. Restaurant and takeaway (May-Oct). Pets are not permitted in rental accommodation or tents. Off site: Public transport from the gate during the summer months. Pub and shop 900 m. Riding 6 km. Golf 12 km. Boating, fishing and sea angling 200 m. Beach (pebble) 500 m.

Open: 1 April - 31 December.

Directions: From the N22, 17 km. east of Killarney, take the R569 south to Kenmare. In Kenmare take R571, Castletownbere road and site is 12 km. GPS: 51.8279, -9.7356

Charges guide

Per unit incl. 2 persons and electricity	€ 22,50
extra person	€ 3,50
child (0-10 yrs)	€ 2,00

BELGIUM – Lombardsijde Middelkerke

Camping De Lombarde

Elisabethlaan 4, B-8434 Lombardsijde Middelkerke (West Flanders)
t: 058 236 839 e: info@delombarde.be
alanrogers.com/BE0560 www.delombarde.be

Accommodation: ☑ Pitch ☑ Mobile home/chalet ☐ Hotel/B&B ☐ Apartment

De Lombarde is a spacious, good value holiday site between Lombardsijde and the coast. It has a pleasant atmosphere and modern buildings. The 380 pitches are set out in level, grassy bays surrounded by shrubs, all with electricity (16A), long leads may be needed. Vehicles are parked in separate car parks. There are many seasonal units and 22 holiday homes, leaving 180 touring pitches. There is a range of activities and an entertainment programme in season. This is a popular holiday area and the site becomes full at peak times. A pleasant stroll takes you into Lombardsijde. There is a tram service from near the site entrance to the town and the beach.

You might like to know

The site operates a tram service to the sandy beach and dunes 500 m. away.

- ☐ **Beach on site**
- ☑ **Beach within 1 km**
- ☑ **Sandy beach**
- ☐ **Blue Flag quality**
- ☐ **Lifeguard** *(high season)*
- ☐ **Sun lounger and/or deckchair hire**
- ☑ **Watersports** *(e.g. sailing or windsurfing)*
- ☐ **Snacks and drinks**
- ☐ **Sunshades/sunbeds**
- ☐ **Dogs allowed** *(on the beach)*

Facilities: Three heated sanitary units are of an acceptable standard, with some washbasins in cubicles. Facilities for disabled visitors (but not for children). Large laundry. Motorcaravan services. Shop, restaurant/bar and takeaway (July/Aug. plus weekends and holidays 1/4-31/8). Tennis. Boules. Fishing lake. TV lounge. Entertainment programme for children. Playground. Internet access (in the bar). ATM. Torch useful. Max. 1 dog. Off site: Beach 400 m. Riding and golf 500 m. Bicycle hire 1 km.

Open: All year.

Directions: Coming from Westende, follow the tramlines. From traffic lights in Lombardsijde, turn left following tramlines into Zeelaan. Continue following tramlines until crossroads and tram stop, turn left into Elisabethlaan. Site is on right after 200 m. GPS: 51.15644, 2.75329

Charges guide

Per unit incl. 1-6 persons and electricity	€ 17,50 - € 31,50
dog (1 per pitch)	€ 2,60

No credit cards.

BELGIUM – De Haan

Camping Ter Duinen

Wenduinsesteenweg 143, B-8421 De Haan (West Flanders)
t: **050 413 593** e: **infolawrence.sansens@scarlet.com**
alanrogers.com/BE0578 www.campingterduinen.be

Accommodation: ☑ Pitch ☑ Mobile home/chalet ☐ Hotel/B&B ☐ Apartment

Ter Duinen is a large, seaside holiday site with 120 pitches for touring and over 700 privately owned static holiday caravans. The pitches are laid out in straight lines with tarmac access roads and the site has three immaculate toilet blocks. Other than a bar and a playing field, the site has little else to offer, but it is only a 400 m. walk to the sea and next door to the site is a large sports complex with a sub-tropical pool and several sporting facilities. Opportunities for riding and golf (18-hole course) are close by. It is possible to hire bicycles in the town. The best places to visit for a day trip are Ostend with the Atlantic Wall from WWII, Knokke (which holds many summer festivals) and Bruges.

You might like to know

The campsite is ideally situated for day trips to Bruges, Knokke and Ostend.

- ☐ **Beach on site**
- ☑ **Beach within 1 km**
- ☑ **Sandy beach**
- ☐ **Blue Flag quality**
- ☐ **Lifeguard** *(high season)*
- ☐ **Sun lounger and/or deckchair hire**
- ☐ **Watersports** *(e.g. sailing or windsurfing)*
- ☐ **Snacks and drinks**
- ☐ **Sunshades/sunbeds**
- ☐ **Dogs allowed** *(on the beach)*

Facilities: Three modern toilet blocks have good fittings, washbasins in cubicles (hot and cold water) and showers (€ 1.20). Baby bath. Facilities for disabled visitors. Laundry facilities with two washing machines and a dryer, irons and ironing boards. Motorcaravan service point. Shop. Snack bar and takeaway. WiFi (charged).
Off site: Bicycle hire and sea with sandy beach 400 m. Riding 1 km. Golf 3 km. Boat launching 6 km. A bus for Bruges stops 200 m. from the site, a tram for the coast 400 m.

Open: 16 March - 15 October.

Directions: On E40 in either direction take exit for De Haan/Jabbeke. About 3 km. south of De Haan, turn at signs for campsites.
GPS: 51.28318, 3.05753

Charges guide

Per unit incl. 2 persons and electricity	€ 17,00 - € 24,00
extra person	€ 2,50
child (under 10 yrs)	€ 2,00
dog	€ 3,00

NETHERLANDS – Katwijk aan Zee

Recreatiecentrum De Noordduinen

Campingweg 1, NL-2221 EW Katwijk aan Zee (Zuid-Holland)
t: 0714 025 295 e: info@noordduinen.nl
alanrogers.com/NL5680 www.noordduinen.nl

Accommodation: ☑ Pitch ☑ Mobile home/chalet ☐ Hotel/B&B ☐ Apartment

This is a large, well managed site surrounded by dunes and sheltered partly by trees and shrubbery, which also separate the various camping areas. The 200 touring pitches are marked and numbered but not divided. All have electricity (10A) and 75 are fully serviced with electricity, water, drainage and TV connection. There are also seasonal pitches and mobile homes for rent. Entertainment is organised in high season for various age groups. A new complex with indoor and outdoor pools, restaurant, small theatre and recreation hall provides a good addition to the site's facilities. Seasonal pitches and mobile homes are mostly away from the touring areas and are unobtrusive. You are escorted to an allocated pitch and sited in a formal layout and cars are parked away from the pitches; however, with the super pitch your car can be parked on the pitch. Bicycles can be hired on site plus the nearby Space Expo is well worth a visit. The beaches are inviting and offer numerous possibilities for long walks and cycling tours.

You might like to know

The broad sandy beaches and sheltered dunes make this a beautiful area ideal for nature lovers and safe for young children.

- ☐ **Beach on site**
- ☑ **Beach within 1 km**
- ☑ **Sandy beach**
- ☐ **Blue Flag quality**
- ☐ **Lifeguard** *(high season)*
- ☐ **Sun lounger and/or deckchair hire**
- ☐ **Watersports** *(e.g. sailing or windsurfing)*
- ☐ **Snacks and drinks**
- ☐ **Sunshades/sunbeds**
- ☐ **Dogs allowed** *(on the beach)*

Facilities: The three sanitary blocks are modern and clean, with washbasins in cabins, a baby room and provision for visitors with disabilities. Laundry. Motorcaravan services. Supermarket with fresh bread daily, bar, restaurant, takeaway (all 1/4-31/10). Recreation room. Swimming pool complex. Play area. Only gas barbecues are permitted. Dogs are not accepted.
Off site: Riding 150 m. Beach and fishing 300 m. Golf 6 km. Katwijk within walking distance.

Open: All year.

Directions: Leave A44 at exit 8 (Leiden - Katwijk) to join N206 to Katwijk. Take Katwijk Noord exit and follow signs to site. GPS: 52.21103, 4.40978

Charges guide

Per unit incl. 2 persons and electricity	€ 28,00 - € 36,00
extra person	€ 4,00

NETHERLANDS – Nieuwvliet

Camping Zonneweelde

Baanstpoldersedijk 1, NL-4504 PS Nieuwvliet (Zeeland)
t: **0117 371 910** e: **info@campingzonneweelde.nl**
alanrogers.com/NL5530 www.campingzonneweelde.nl

Accommodation: ☑ Pitch ☑ Mobile home/chalet ☐ Hotel/B&B ☐ Apartment

This family run site, only ten minutes walk from kilometers of wide, sandy beaches, is ideal for family holidays. In addition to pitches for 160 touring units, the site offers a wide range of chalets (20), mobile homes (200) and cabins (2), plus places for 50 seasonal caravans. Electricity connections (10A) are available throughout. Motorcaravans and twin axle caravans are not accepted. The Natural Reserve of Het Zwin is nearby (bird watching) and many interesting villages are in the area. Public transport operates in July and August from Breskens, via Sluis to visit Brugge in Belgium.

You might like to know

There's plenty of great children's entertainment here, particularly in high season, based at the Twinkelhuis.

- ☐ **Beach on site**
- ☑ **Beach within 1 km**
- ☑ **Sandy beach**
- ☑ **Blue Flag quality**
- ☑ **Lifeguard** *(high season)*
- ☑ **Sun lounger and/or deckchair hire**
- ☐ **Watersports** *(e.g. sailing or windsurfing)*
- ☑ **Snacks and drinks**
- ☑ **Sunshades/sunbeds**
- ☑ **Dogs allowed** *(on the beach)*

Facilities: A modern, heated and well maintained sanitary building provides roomy adjustable showers and some washbasins in cabins. Children's bathroom. Also one small sanitary block with 8 WC and 4 wash cabins. Both blocks have laundry facilities. Restaurant with takeaway. Supermarket. Swimming pool (guarded in July/Aug) and separate pool for toddlers. Play areas and sports field. Bicycle hire.

Open: 3 April - 30 October.

Directions: From Westerscheldetunnel, turn right at roundabout to Breskens-Hoek-Oostburg. At Schoondijke roundabout follow signs for Breskens/Groede, turn left at first traffic lights to Groede/Nieuwvliet then right at first roundabout in Nieuwvliet. Site is signed. From Belgium: take N49 to Kaprijke and Breskens, entering NL at IJzendijke. At traffic light in Breskens turn left to Groede/Cadzand, and follow site signs.
GPS: 51.382207, 3.458188

Charges guide

Per unit incl. 2 persons and electricity	€ 16,00 - € 35,00
extra person (over 2 yrs)	€ 5,00
dog (max 1)	€ 2,50

Erkemederstrand Camping Horeca

Erkemederweg 79, NL-3896 LB Zeewolde (Flevoland)
t: 0365 228 421 e: info@erkemederstrand.nl
alanrogers.com/NL6200 www.erkemederstrand.nl

Accommodation: ☑ Pitch ☑ Mobile home/chalet ☐ Hotel/B&B ☐ Apartment

The Erkemederstrand (the beach of Erkemede) is a leisure park at Flevoland, with direct access to the Nuldernauw, a sandy beach, water and forest. It provides a campsite for families, a marina, an area for youngsters to camp, a camping area for groups and a recreation area for day visitors. The campsite itself is divided into two areas: one before the dyke at the waterfront and one behind the dyke. The pitches are spacious (around 125 sq.m) and all have electricity, water and drainage. The focal point of the site and marina is the beach restaurant, De Jutter. This restaurant offers a varied menu for more formal dining, as well as catering for snacks, takeaway, ice creams or a cold beer on the terrace. There is plenty to do on the campsite, including a Red Indian village for the children where they can build huts, a children's farm and an extended entertainment programme. Obviously with the proximity of the lake there are many opportunities for watersports.

Special offers

All campsite visitors have free, unlimited access to the 3 km. long beach.

You might like to know

One of the longest stretches of beach in Flevoland, located in a freshwater area with grassy terrain. There is plenty to do – beach football, volleyball, minigolf, a playground and even a military truck to explore.

- ☑ Beach on site
- ☐ Beach within 1 km
- ☑ Sandy beach
- ☐ Blue Flag quality
- ☐ Lifeguard *(high season)*
- ☐ Sun lounger and/or deckchair hire
- ☑ Watersports *(e.g. sailing or windsurfing)*
- ☑ Snacks and drinks
- ☐ Sunshades/sunbeds
- ☑ Dogs allowed *(on the beach)*

Facilities: Four neat and clean toilet blocks (access by key; exclusively for campers). Washbasins in cabins, showers and family bathrooms (free hot water). Dishwashing and laundry facilities in heated buildings. Shop for basic provisions. Bar, restaurant and takeaway. Several play areas and children's farm. Watersports facilities and lake swimming. Football pitch. Minigolf. Bicycle hire. Extended entertainment programme. Off site: Golf and riding 11 km.

Open: 1 April - 30 October.

Directions: From the A28 (Utrecht - Zwolle) take exit 9 (Nijkerk/Almere) and follow N301 to Zeewolde. Cross the bridge and turn right following signs to site. From Amsterdam/Almere, take exit 5 and follow N27 to Zeewolde; this road changes into the N305. Then take N301 to Nijkerk. From the bridge turn right and follow signs to site. GPS: 52.27021, 5.48871

Charges guide

Per unit incl. 2 persons and electricity	€ 25,75 - € 32,00
extra person	€ 3,00
dog	€ 2,00

NETHERLANDS – Cadzand

Molecaten Park Hoogduin

Zwartepolderweg 1, NL-4506 HT Cadzand (Zeeland)
t: **0117 391 235** e: **info@campinghoogduin.nl**
alanrogers.com/NL6937 www.molecaten.nl/hoogduin

Accommodation: ☑ Pitch ☑ Mobile home/chalet ☐ Hotel/B&B ☐ Apartment

Hoogduin is a member of the Molecaten Group and can be reached in less than two hours drive from Calais. The location of this site is imposing, and, as its name suggests, it can be found within high dunes (Hoogduin). Just over the dunes, there is a broad sandy beach with a panoramic view over the site and the surrounding area. This beach is well known as one of the cleanest in the Netherlands, and slopes gently into the sea. Pitches are large and grassy, and are mostly equipped with electricity (4-14A). They are divided by high trees and shrubs. This is a very rural region, known as Zeeuws-Vlaanderen. It is an area which combines the maritime culture of Zeeland with the fine gourmet cuisine of Belgian Flanders. Zeeland is renowned for its mussels, and combined with Flemish chips, you have one of the country's most popular meals. The medieval town of Bruges, once the chief trading town of the world, is only 20 km. away.

You might like to know

Fantastic position right behind the dunes and within walking distance of the beach. Rent one of our beach huts and experience the ultimate in seaside luxury!

- ☑ **Beach on site**
- ☐ **Beach within 1 km**
- ☑ **Sandy beach**
- ☐ **Blue Flag quality**
- ☐ **Lifeguard** *(high season)*
- ☐ **Sun lounger and/or deckchair hire**
- ☐ **Watersports** *(e.g. sailing or windsurfing)*
- ☑ **Snacks and drinks**
- ☑ **Sunshades/sunbeds**
- ☐ **Dogs allowed** *(on the beach)*

Facilities: Restaurant with pub and terrace, takeaway food. Supermarket. Play area with trampoline. Table tennis. Volleyball. Games room. Activity programme. Bicycle hire. Mobile homes and chalets for rent. Off site: Sandy beach (adjacent). Cadzand-Bad 2 km. Knokke 7 km. Bruges 20 km.

Open: 1 April - 1 November.

Directions: From the south take E40 motorway (in Belgium) to Oostkamp take E403 to Brugge (Bruges) and Knokke-Heist. Follow this road into The Netherlands following directions to Cadzand. Continue on N674. At the T-junction (at coast) turn right and you will find the site after 1 km. GPS: 51.38453, 3.41397

Charges guide

Per unit incl. 2 persons, water and electricity	€ 17,50 - € 30,50
extra person	€ 3,90
child (2-10 yrs)	€ 2,90
dog	€ 3,90

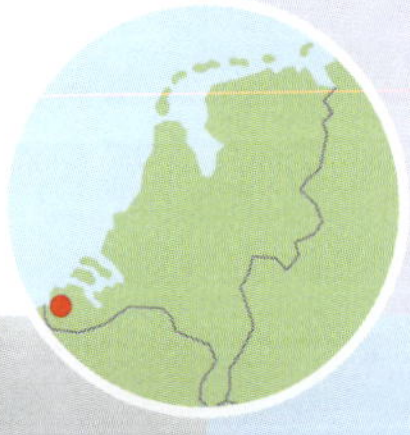

NETHERLANDS – Noordwelle

Camping De Zeeuwse Kust

Helleweg 8, NL-4326 LJ Noordwelle (Zeeland)
t: **0111 468 282** e: **info@dezeeuwsekust.eu**
alanrogers.com/NL6948 www.dezeeuwsekust.eu

Accommodation: ☑ Pitch ☑ Mobile home/chalet ☐ Hotel/B&B ☐ Apartment

Camping De Zeeuwse Kust opened in April 2007. This new site is positioned on the island Schouwen-Duivenland, at the foot of the dunes and just five minutes from the well known seaside resort of Renesse. This site has 168 pitches which are spacious and comfortable. The luxurious sanitary facilities are heated and also provide facilities for disabled visitors. Some pitches have private sanitary provision. The sea offers plenty of opportunities for kite surfing, windsurfing and sailing and there are also plenty of walks possible through the dunes. For those who cannot sail but would like to learn, there is a sailing school where you can have lessons. Whether you just want relaxation, something for the children, the seaside, or activities, you will find these all at Camping De Zeeuwse Kust. The recreation team organises several activities for children all year, such as treasure hunts, games, sports and arts and crafts afternoons.

You might like to know

De Zeeuwse Kust is just 250 m. from a North Sea beach. Nearby is a stretch of sand where you can kite surf.

- ☐ **Beach on site**
- ☑ **Beach within 1 km**
- ☑ **Sandy beach**
- ☑ **Blue Flag quality**
- ☐ **Lifeguard** *(high season)*
- ☐ **Sun lounger and/or deckchair hire**
- ☑ **Watersports** *(e.g. sailing or windsurfing)*
- ☑ **Snacks and drinks**
- ☐ **Sunshades/sunbeds**
- ☑ **Dogs allowed** *(on the beach)*

Facilities: New, first-class sanitary building providing showers, washbasins, private cabins, family shower rooms and other facilities for children and disabled visitors. Launderette. Cooking facilities. Shop. Fresh bread (May-Sept). Excellent heated swimming pool. Play areas (indoors and outdoors). Entertainment team. Barbecue area. First aid post. WiFi.
Off site: Riding 500 m. Golf 7 km. Boat launching 7.5 km.

Open: All year (with most facilities).

Directions: From the A15 take exit 12 towards Middelburg. Follow the N57 through Ouddorp and then turn right on the N652. Immediately turn left for the N651 and follow to Nordwelle. Site is well signed. GPS: 51.73205, 3.79443

Charges guide

Per unit incl. 2 persons, electricity, water and drainage	€ 19,00 - € 45,00
extra person (over 2 yrs)	€ 5,75
dog	€ 4,00

No credit cards.

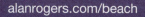

GERMANY – Wulfen auf Fehmarn

Camping Wulfener Hals

Wulfener Hals Weg, D-23769 Wulfen auf Fehmarn (Schleswig-Holstein)
t: **043 718 6280** e: **camping@wulfenerhals.de**
alanrogers.com/DE3003 www.wulfenerhals.de

Accommodation: ☑ Pitch ☑ Mobile home/chalet ☐ Hotel/B&B ☐ Apartment

This a top class, all year round site suitable as a stopover or as a base for a longer stay. Attractively situated by the sea, it is a large, mature site (34 hectares) and is well maintained. It has over 800 individual pitches (half for touring) of up to 160 sq.m. in glades. Some are separated by bushes providing shade in the older parts, less so in the newer areas nearer the sea. There are many hardstandings and all pitches have electricity, water and drainage. A separate area has been developed for motorcaravans. It provides 60 extra large pitches, all with electricity, water and drainage, and some with TV aerial points, together with a new toilet block. There is much to do for young and old alike at Wulfener Hals, with a new heated outdoor pool and paddling pool (unsupervised), although the sea is naturally popular as well. The site also has many sporting facilities including its own golf courses and schools for watersports. A member of Leading Campings Group.

You might like to know

Some of the water-based activities available include sailing with catamarans, surfing and kite-surfing, diving courses and wreck-diving with professionals.

- ☑ **Beach on site**
- ☐ **Beach within 1 km**
- ☑ **Sandy beach**
- ☐ **Blue Flag quality**
- ☑ **Lifeguard** *(high season)*
- ☐ **Sun lounger and/or deckchair hire**
- ☑ **Watersports** *(e.g. sailing or windsurfing)*
- ☑ **Snacks and drinks**
- ☐ **Sunshades/sunbeds**
- ☑ **Dogs allowed** *(on the beach)*

Facilities: Five heated sanitary buildings have first class facilities including showers, open washbasins and private cabins. Family bathrooms for rent. Facilities for children and disabled campers. Beauty facilities. Laundry. Motorcaravan services. Shop, bar, restaurants and takeaway (April-Oct). Swimming pool (May-Oct). Sauna. Solarium. Jacuzzi. Sailing, catamaran, windsurfing and diving schools. Boat slipway. Golf courses. Riding. Fishing. Archery. Entertainment programmes for children of all ages. Bicycle hire. Catamaran hire.
Off site: Naturist beach 500 m. Minimarket 2 km.

Open: All year.

Directions: From Hamburg take A1/E47 north direction Puttgarden, after crossing the bridge to Fehmarn first exit to the right to Avendorf. In Avendorf turn left and follow the signs for Wulfen and the site. GPS: 54.40805, 11.17374

Charges guide

Per unit incl. 2 persons and electricity	€ 14,60 - € 42,11
extra person	€ 4,10 - € 8,60
child (2-18 yrs)	€ 2,30 - € 7,40
dog	€ 1,00 - € 7,50

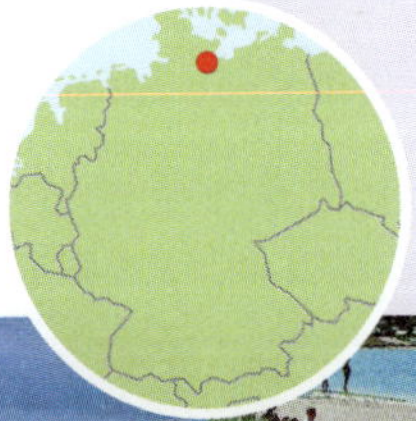

GERMANY – Fehmarn

Strandcamping Wallnau

Wallnau 1, D-23769 Fehmarn (Schleswig-Holstein)
t: 043 729 456 e: wallnau@strandcamping.de
alanrogers.com/DE3007 www.strandcamping.de

Accommodation: ☑ Pitch ☑ Mobile home/chalet ☐ Hotel/B&B ☐ Apartment

With direct beach access and protected from the wind by a dyke, this family site is on Germany's second largest island (since 1963 joined to the Baltic sea coast by a bridge). This is a quiet location on the western part of Fehmarn island in close proximity to a large bird sanctuary. Of the 800 pitches, 400 are for touring, all with electricity and on level grass areas arranged in alleys and separated by hedges. The island is low lying, ideal for leisurely walking or cycle riding, especially along the track that runs along the top of the dyke. The beach is a mixture of sand and pebbles and in summer lifeguards are on duty. The southern part is a naturist area. For those with an ornithological interest, the bird sanctuary with over 80 species is worth visiting. Swimming, sailing and diving are possible in the sea and there is a windsurfing school. For those who prefer dry land there is pony riding for children and a riding school. In summer there are entertainment programmes for children and courses for adults; twice a week there are film shows.

You might like to know

The site boasts a specialist kite- and windsurfing school, its own dive centre and riding stables. Additionally, the site is located next to the Wallnau bird sanctuary.

- ☑ **Beach on site**
- ☐ **Beach within 1 km**
- ☐ **Sandy beach**
- ☐ **Blue Flag quality**
- ☑ **Lifeguard** *(high season)*
- ☐ **Sun lounger and/or deckchair hire**
- ☑ **Watersports** *(e.g. sailing or windsurfing)*
- ☐ **Snacks and drinks**
- ☐ **Sunshades/sunbeds**
- ☐ **Dogs allowed** *(on the beach)*

Facilities: Heated sanitary blocks (cleaning variable) provide free showers. Child-size toilets and showers. Baby rooms. Facilities for disabled visitors. Laundry facilities. Motorcaravan service points. Shop. Bar, restaurant and snack bar. Open-air stage and soundproofed disco. Health/cure centre, solarium and sauna. Archery. Watersports. Minigolf. Internet café. Beach fishing. Riding. WiFi (charged). Off site: Boat launching 6 km. Golf 15 km.

Open: 27 March - 25 October.

Directions: After crossing the bridge follow road to Landkirchen and Petersdorf. From Petersdorf site is signed. It is 4 km. northwest of the town. GPS: 54.48761, 11.0186

Charges guide

Per unit incl. 2 persons and electricity	€ 18,00 - € 35,30
child (under 17 yrs)	€ 2,00 - € 6,30
extra person	€ 4,00 - € 7,40

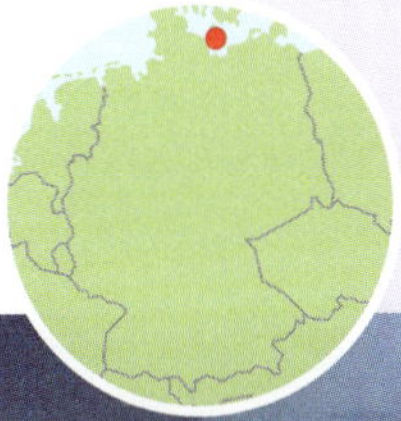

DENMARK – Blavand

Hvidbjerg Strand Camping

Hvidbjerg Strandvej 27, DK-6857 Blavand (Ribe)
t: **75 27 90 40** e: **info@hvidbjerg.dk**
alanrogers.com/DK2010 www.hvidbjerg.dk

Accommodation: ☑ Pitch ☑ Mobile home/chalet ☐ Hotel/B&B ☐ Apartment

A family owned TopCamp holiday site, Hvidbjerg Strand is on the west coast near Blåvands Huk, 43 km. from Esbjerg. It is a high quality, seaside site with a wide range of amenities. Most of the 570 pitches have electricity (6/10A) and the 130 'comfort' pitches also have water, drainage and satellite TV. To the rear of the site, 70 new, fully serviced pitches have been developed, some up to 250 sq. m. and 16 with private sanitary facilities. Most pitches are individual and divided by hedges, in rows on flat sandy grass, with areas also divided by small trees and hedges. On-site leisure facilities include supervised playrooms with Lego, computers, video games, TV, etc. The impressive, tropical style indoor pool complex has stalactite caves and a 70 m. water chute; the 'black hole' with sounds and lights, water slides, spa baths, Turkish bath and a sauna. A Blue Flag beach and windsurfing school are adjacent to the site and the town offers a full activity programme during high season. A member of Leading Campings Group.

You might like to know

The special conditions here are due to the reef known as 'Horns Reef', which stretches 40 km. into the North Sea creating a lagoon on its south side.

- ☑ **Beach on site**
- ☐ **Beach within 1 km**
- ☑ **Sandy beach**
- ☑ **Blue Flag quality**
- ☐ **Lifeguard** *(high season)*
- ☐ **Sun lounger and/or deckchair hire**
- ☑ **Watersports** *(e.g. sailing or windsurfing)*
- ☐ **Snacks and drinks**
- ☐ **Sunshades/sunbeds**
- ☐ **Dogs allowed** *(on the beach)*

Facilities: Five superb toilet units include washbasins (many in cubicles), roomy showers, spa baths, suites for disabled visitors, family bathrooms, kitchens and laundry facilities. The most recent units include a children's bathroom decorated with dinosaurs and Disney characters, and racing car baby baths. Motorcaravan services. Supermarket. Café/restaurant. TV rooms. Pool complex, solarium and sauna. Play areas. Supervised play rooms (09.00-16.00 daily). Barbecue areas. Minigolf. Riding (Western style). Fishing. Dog showers. ATM machine.
Off site: Legoland 70 km.

Open: 18 March - 23 October.

Directions: From Varde take roads 181/431 to Blåvand. Site is signed left on entering the town (mind speed bump on town boundary).
GPS: 55.54600, 8.13507

Charges guide

Per unit incl. 2 persons and electricity	DKK 239 - 404
extra person	DKK 77
child (0-11 yrs)	DKK 57
dog	DKK 27

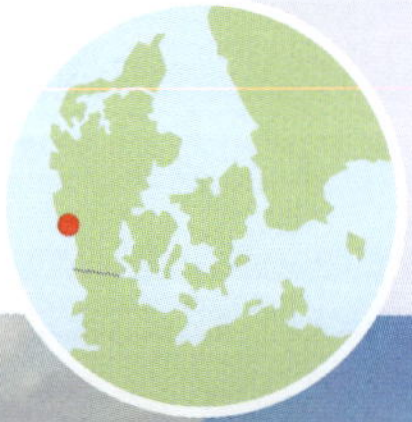

DENMARK – Fjerritslev

Klim Strand Camping

Havvejen 167, Klim Strand, DK-9690 Fjerritslev (Nordjylland)
t: 98 22 53 40 e: ksc@klim-strand.dk
alanrogers.com/DK2170 www.klim-strand.dk

Accommodation: ☑ Pitch ☑ Mobile home/chalet ☐ Hotel/B&B ☐ Apartment

A large family holiday site right beside the sea, Klim Strand is a paradise for children. It is a privately owned TopCamp site with a full complement of quality facilities, including its own fire engine and trained staff. The site has 460 numbered touring pitches, all with electricity (10A), laid out in rows, many divided by trees and hedges with shade in parts. Some 220 of these are fully serviced with electricity, water, drainage and TV hook-up. On-site activities include an outdoor water slide complex, an indoor pool, tennis courts and pony riding (all free). A wellness spa centre is a recent addition. For children there are numerous play areas, an adventure playground with aerial cable ride and a roller skating area. There is a kayak school and a large bouncy castle for toddlers. Live music and dancing are organised twice a week in high season. Suggested excursions include trips to offshore islands, visits to local potteries, a brewery museum and bird watching on the Bygholm Vejle. A member of Leading Campings Group.

You might like to know

There is a bird reserve nearby and several inland lakes with fishing trips available.

- ☑ Beach on site
- ☐ Beach within 1 km
- ☑ Sandy beach
- ☑ Blue Flag quality
- ☐ Lifeguard *(high season)*
- ☐ Sun lounger and/or deckchair hire
- ☐ Watersports *(e.g. sailing or windsurfing)*
- ☐ Snacks and drinks
- ☐ Sunshades/sunbeds
- ☐ Dogs allowed *(on the beach)*

Facilities: Two good, large, heated toilet blocks are central, with spacious showers and some washbasins in cubicles. Separate children's room. Baby rooms. Bathrooms for families (some charged) and disabled visitors. Two smaller units are by reception and beach. Laundry. Well equipped kitchens and barbecue areas. TV lounges. Motorcaravan services. Pizzeria. Supermarket, restaurant and bar (all season). Pool complex. Sauna, solariums, whirlpool bath, hairdressing rooms, fitness room. Wellness centre. Internet café. TV rental. Play areas. Crèche. Bicycle hire. Cabins to rent.
Off site: Golf 10 km. Boat launching 25 km.

Open: 26 March - 24 October.

Directions: Turn off Thisted - Fjerritslev 11 road to Klim from where site is signed.
GPS: 57.133333, 9.166667

Charges guide

Per unit incl. 2 persons and electricity	DKK 305 - 355
extra person	DKK 75
child (1-11 yrs)	DKK 55
dog	DKK 25

DENMARK – Fåborg

Bøjden Strand Ferie Park

Bøjden Landevej 12, Bøjden, DK-5600 Fåborg (Fyn)
t: **63 60 63 60** e: **info@bojden.dk**
alanrogers.com/DK2200 www.bojden.dk

Accommodation: ☑ Pitch ☑ Mobile home/chalet ☐ Hotel/B&B ☐ Apartment

Bøjden is located in one of the most beautiful corners of southwest Fyn (Funen in English) known as the Garden of Denmark. Bøjden is a delightful, well equipped site with just a hedge separating it from the beach. It is suitable for an entire holiday, while remaining a very good centre for excursions. Arranged in rows on mainly level, grassy terraces and divided into groups by hedges and some trees, many pitches have sea views as the site slopes gently down from the road. The 295 pitches (210 for touring) all have electricity (10A) and include 65 new, fully serviced pitches (water, drainage and TV aerial point). Four special motorcaravan pitches also have water and waste points. There are indoor and outdoor pools, the latter with a paddling pool and sun terrace open during suitable weather conditions. Everyone will enjoy the beach (Blue Flag) for swimming, boating and watersports. The water is too shallow for shore fishing but boat trips can be arranged.

You might like to know

The campsite has its own kayak school, a modern indoor and outdoor pool complex and is convenient for day trips to Fåborg, a wonderful old seaport.

- ☑ **Beach on site**
- ☐ **Beach within 1 km**
- ☐ **Sandy beach**
- ☑ **Blue Flag quality**
- ☐ **Lifeguard** *(high season)*
- ☐ **Sun lounger and/or deckchair hire**
- ☑ **Watersports** *(e.g. sailing or windsurfing)*
- ☐ **Snacks and drinks**
- ☐ **Sunshades/sunbeds**
- ☐ **Dogs allowed** *(on the beach)*

Facilities: The superb quality, central toilet block includes washbasins in cubicles, controllable showers, family bathrooms (some with whirlpools and double showers), baby room and excellent facilities for disabled visitors. Well appointed kitchen and laundry. A new unit serves a recent extension to the site. An older unit near reception provides extra facilities and a further kitchen. Motorcaravan services. Supermarket. Licensed restaurant. Takeaway. Indoor and outdoor swimming pools. Solarium. Well equipped, fenced toddler play area and separate adventure playground. TV and games rooms. Internet café and WiFi. Barbecue area. Fishing. Minigolf.
Off site: Beach adjacent. Bicycle hire and riding 10 km. Golf 12 km.

Open: 14 March - 20 October.

Directions: From Fåborg follow 8 road to Bøjden and site is on right 500 m. before ferry terminal (from Fynshav). GPS: 55.105289, 10.107808

Charges guide

Per person	DKK 67
child (0-11 yrs)	DKK 45
pitch	DKK 10 - 100
electricity	DKK 31

DENMARK – Faxe

TopCamp Feddet

Feddet 12, DK-4640 Faxe (Sjælland)
t: 56 72 52 06 e: info@feddetcamping.dk
alanrogers.com/DK2255 www.feddetcamping.dk

Accommodation: ☑ Pitch ☑ Mobile home/chalet ☐ Hotel/B&B ☐ Apartment

This interesting, spacious site with ecological principles is located on the Baltic coast. It has a fine, white, sandy beach (Blue Flag) which runs the full length of one side, with the Præstø fjord on the opposite side of the peninsula. There are 413 pitches for touring units, generally on sandy grass, with mature pine trees giving adequate shade. All have 10A electricity and 20 are fully serviced. Two recently constructed sanitary buildings which have been specially designed, are clad with larch panels from sustainable local trees and are insulated with flax mats. They have natural ventilation, with ventilators controlled by sensors for heat, humidity and smell. Shaped blades on the roof increase ventilation on windy days. All this saves power and provides a comfortable climate inside. Heating, by a wood chip furnace (backed up by a rapeseed oil furnace), is CO^2 neutral and replaces 40,000 litres of heating oil annually. Rainwater is used for toilet flushing, but showers and basins are supplied from the normal mains.

You might like to know

For something completely different, why not try your hand at abseiling?

- ☑ Beach on site
- ☐ Beach within 1 km
- ☑ Sandy beach
- ☑ Blue Flag quality
- ☐ Lifeguard *(high season)*
- ☐ Sun lounger and/or deckchair hire
- ☐ Watersports *(e.g. sailing or windsurfing)*
- ☐ Snacks and drinks
- ☐ Sunshades/sunbeds
- ☐ Dogs allowed *(on the beach)*

Facilities: Both sanitary buildings are impressive, equipped to a very high standard. Family bathrooms (with twin showers), complete suites for small children and babies. Facilities for disabled campers. Laundry. Kitchens, dining room and TV lounge. Excellent motorcaravan service point. Well stocked licensed shop. Licensed bistro and takeaway (1/5-20/10 but weekends only outside peak season). Minigolf. Games room. Indoor playroom and several playgrounds for all ages. Event camp for children. Pet zoo. WiFi. Massage. Watersports. Fishing. Off site: Abseiling and pool. Amusement park.

Open: All year.

Directions: From south on E47/55 take exit 38 towards Præsto. Turn north on 209 road towards Faxe and from Vindbyholt follow site signs. From the north on E47/55 take exit 37 east towards Faxe. Just before Faxe turn south on 209 road and from Vindbyholt, site signs.
GPS: 55.17497, 12.10203

Charges guide

Per unit incl. 2 persons and electricity	DKK 250 - 323
extra person	DKK 72
child (0-11 yrs)	DKK 50 - 105
dog	DKK 20

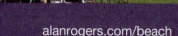

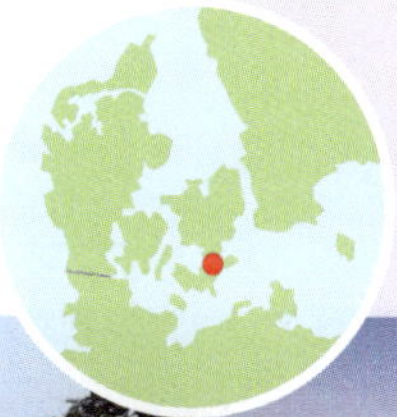

SWEDEN – Torekov

First Camp Båstad-Torekov

Flymossa Vagen 5, S-260 93 Torekov (Skåne Län)
t: **043 136 4525** e: **torekov@firstcamp.se**
alanrogers.com/SW2640 www.firstcamp.se

Accommodation: ☑ Pitch ☑ Mobile home/chalet ☐ Hotel/B&B ☐ Apartment

Part of the First Camp chain, this site is 500 m. from the fishing village of Torekov, 14 km. west of the home of the Swedish tennis WCT Open at Båstad, on the stretch of coastline between Malmö and Göteborg. Useful en route from the most southerly ports, it is a very good site and worthy of a longer stay for relaxation. It has 535 large pitches (390 for touring units), all numbered and marked, mainly in attractive natural woodland, with some on more open ground close to the shore. Of these, 300 have electricity (10A) and cable TV, 77 also having water and drainage. The modern reception complex is professionally run and is also home for a good shop, a snack bar, restaurant, and pizzeria. The spacious site covers quite a large area and there is a cycle track along the shore to the bathing beach. Games for children are organised in high season and there is an outdoor stage for musical entertainment and dancing (also in high season). This well run site is a pleasant place to stay.

You might like to know

At nearby Torekov, fishing boats are available to hire. Alternatively, take a short boat ride to Halland Vadero for a seal safari or to swim in the safe, shallow water.

- ☑ **Beach on site**
- ☐ **Beach within 1 km**
- ☑ **Sandy beach**
- ☐ **Blue Flag quality**
- ☐ **Lifeguard** *(high season)*
- ☐ **Sun lounger and/or deckchair hire**
- ☑ **Watersports** *(e.g. sailing or windsurfing)*
- ☐ **Snacks and drinks**
- ☐ **Sunshades/sunbeds**
- ☐ **Dogs allowed** *(on the beach)*

Facilities: Three very good sanitary blocks with facilities for babies and disabled visitors. Laundry. Cooking facilities and dishwashing. Motorcaravan service point. Bar. Restaurant, pizzeria and snack bar with takeaway (15/6-5/8). Shop and kiosk. Minigolf. Sports fields. Play areas and adventure park for children. Bicycle hire. TV room. Beach. Fishing. WiFi on all pitches. Off site: Games, music and entertainment in high season. Tennis close by. Golf 1 km. Riding 3 km.

Open: 15 April - 25 September.

Directions: From E6 Malmö - Göteborg road take Torekov/Båstad exit and follow signs for 20 km. towards Torekov. Site is signed 1 km. before village on right. GPS: 56.43097, 12.64055

Charges guide

Per unit incl. 4 persons and electricity	SEK 190 - 305

SWEDEN – Färjestaden

Krono Camping Saxnäs

S-386 95 Färjestaden (Kalmar Län)
t: **048 535 700** e: **info@kcsaxnas.se**
alanrogers.com/SW2680 www.kcsaxnas.se

Accommodation: ☑ Pitch ☑ Mobile home/chalet ☐ Hotel/B&B ☐ Apartment

Well placed for touring Sweden's Riviera and the fascinating and beautiful island of Öland, this family run site, part of the Krono group, has 420 marked and numbered touring pitches. Arranged in rows on open, well kept grassland dotted with a few trees, all have electricity (10/16A), 320 have TV connections and 112 also have water. An unmarked area without electricity can accommodate around 60 tents. The site has about 130 long stay units and cabins for rent. The sandy beach slopes very gently and is safe for children. Reception is efficient and friendly with good English spoken. In 2009 an outdoor heated pool and a children's pool were built at the entrance to the site. In high season children's games are organised and dances are held twice weekly, with other activities on other evenings. Nearby attractions include the 7 km. long Öland road bridge and the 400 old windmills on the island (in the 19th century there were 2,000). The southern tip of Öland, Ottenby, is a paradise for bird watchers.

You might like to know

The gently sloping beach is safe for children and is cleaned daily. Youngsters will enjoy the Öland Animal and Amusement Park, just 3 km. away.

- ☑ **Beach on site**
- ☐ **Beach within 1 km**
- ☑ **Sandy beach**
- ☑ **Blue Flag quality**
- ☐ **Lifeguard** *(high season)*
- ☐ **Sun lounger and/or deckchair hire**
- ☐ **Watersports** *(e.g. sailing or windsurfing)*
- ☐ **Snacks and drinks**
- ☐ **Sunshades/sunbeds**
- ☐ **Dogs allowed** *(on the beach)*

Facilities: Three heated sanitary blocks provide a good supply of roomy shower cubicles, washbasins, some washbasin/WC suites and WCs. Facilities for babies and disabled visitors. Well-equipped laundry room. Good kitchen with cookers, microwaves and dishwasher (free), and sinks. Hot water is free. Gas supplies. Motorcaravan services. Shop (1/5-30/8). Pizzeria, licensed restaurant and café (all 1/5-30/8). Bar (1/7-31/7). Outdoor heated swimming pool (15/5-22/8). Playgrounds. Bouncy castle. Boules. Canoe hire. Bicycle hire. Minigolf. Family entertainment and activities. Football. Off site: Golf 500 m. Riding 2 km. Fishing 4km.

Open: 16 April - 26 September.

Directions: Cross Öland road bridge from Kalmar on road no. 137. Take exit for Öland Djurpark/Saxnäs, then follow campsite signs. Site is just north of the end of the bridge. GPS: 56.68727, 16.48182

Charges guide

Per unit incl. electricity	SEK 165 - 330

SWEDEN – Byxelkrok

Krono Camping Böda Sand

S-380 75 Byxelkrok (Kalmar Län)
t: 048 522 200 e: bodasand@kronocampingoland.se
alanrogers.com/SW2690 www.kronocampingoland.se

Accommodation: ☑ Pitch ☑ Mobile home/chalet ☐ Hotel/B&B ☐ Apartment

Krono Camping Böda Sand is beautifully situated at the northern end of the island of Öland and is one of Sweden's largest and most modern campsites. Most of the 1,300 pitches have electricity (10/16A) and TV connections, 130 have water and waste water drainage. The pitches and 123 cabins for rent are spread out in a pine forest, very close to the fabulous 10 km. long, white sand beach. Here you will also find kiosks, a restaurant, toilets and beach showers, and a relaxation centre with an indoor/outdoor pool. The reception, the toilet blocks and the services at this site are excellent and comprehensive. Entertainment and activities for children and adults are very extensive. There are more than 90 different items to choose from every week during high season. For exercise, there are tennis and badminton courts, trim trails, a football pitch and a nine-hole golf course, par 58, in the forest. Nearby attractions are the lighthouse at the northern tip of Öland, the Troll forest and the lime stone natural sculptures at Byerum.

You might like to know

The white sandy beach is cleaned daily. The site offers diving lessons in the pool in high season.

- ☑ **Beach on site**
- ☐ **Beach within 1 km**
- ☑ **Sandy beach**
- ☐ **Blue Flag quality**
- ☐ **Lifeguard** *(high season)*
- ☐ **Sun lounger and/or deckchair hire**
- ☑ **Watersports** *(e.g. sailing or windsurfing)*
- ☑ **Snacks and drinks**
- ☐ **Sunshades/sunbeds**
- ☐ **Dogs allowed** *(on the beach)*

Facilities: Seven heated sanitary blocks provide a good supply of roomy shower cubicles, washbasins, some washbasin suites and WCs. Facilities for babies and disabled visitors (key at reception). Well equipped laundry rooms. Excellent kitchens with cookers, ovens, microwaves, dishwashers (free) and sinks. Motorcaravan services. Supermarket and bakery. Pizzeria, café, pub and restaurant. Takeaway. Bicycle hire, pedal cars and pedal boat hire. WiFi. Minigolf. 9-hole golf course. Indoor/outdoor swimming pool (on the beach). Trim trails. Family entertainment and activities.

Open: 1 May - 1 October.

Directions: From Kalmar cross the Öland road bridge on road no. 137. On Öland follow road no. 136 towards Borgholm and Byxelkrok. Turn left at the roundabout north of Böda and follow the campsite signs to Krono camping Böda Sand. GPS: 57.27436, 17.04851

Charges guide

Per pitch	SEK 155 - 235
incl. electricity	SEK 195 - 285

FINLAND – Oulu

Nallikari Camping

Leiritie 10, FIN-90510 Oulu (Oulu)
t: **044 703 1353** e: **nallikari.camping@ouka.fi**
alanrogers.com/FI2970 **www.nallikari.fi**

Accommodation: ☑ Pitch ☑ Mobile home/chalet ☐ Hotel/B&B ☐ Apartment

This is probably one of the best sites in Scandinavia, set in a recreational wooded area alongside a sandy beach on the banks of the Baltic Sea, with the added bonus of the adjacent Eden Spa complex. Nallikari provides 200 pitches with electricity (175 also have water supply and drainage), plus an additional 78 cottages to rent, 28 of which are suitable for winter occupation. Oulu is a modern town, about 160 km. south of the Arctic Circle, that enjoys long, sunny and dry summer days. The Baltic however is frozen for many weeks in the winter and then the sun barely rises for two months. In early June the days are very long with the sun setting at about 23.30 and rising at 01.30! Nallikari, to the west of Oulu, is 3 km. along purpose-built cycle paths and the town has much to offer. Nordic walking, with or without roller blades, seems to be a recreational pastime for Finns of all ages! You might even be tempted to buy a pair of these long brightly coloured walking sticks yourself!

You might like to know

Activities on the beach include beach volley-ball, and there are beach tennis courts nearby.

- ☑ **Beach on site**
- ☐ **Beach within 1 km**
- ☑ **Sandy beach**
- ☐ **Blue Flag quality**
- ☐ **Lifeguard** *(high season)*
- ☐ **Sun lounger and/or deckchair hire**
- ☐ **Watersports** *(e.g. sailing or windsurfing)*
- ☐ **Snacks and drinks**
- ☐ **Sunshades/sunbeds**
- ☐ **Dogs allowed** *(on the beach)*

Facilities: The modern shower/WC blocks also provide male and female saunas, kitchen and launderette facilities. Facilities for disabled visitors. Motorcaravan service point. Playground. Reception with café/restaurant (June-Aug), souvenir and grocery shop. TV room. WiFi. Bicycle hire. Off site: The adjacent Eden Centre provides excellent modern spa facilities where you can enjoy a day under the glass-roofed pool with its jacuzzis, saunas, Turkish baths and an Irish bath. Fishing 5 km. Golf 15 km.

Open: All year.

Directions: Leave road 4/E75 at junction with road 20 and head west down Kiertotie. Site well signed, Nallikari Eden, but continue on, just after traffic lights, cross a bridge and take the second on the right. Just before the Eden Centre turn right towards Leiritie and reception.
GPS: 65.02973, 25.41793

Charges guide

Per unit incl. 2 persons	€ 10,00 - € 18,00
extra person	€ 4,00
child (under 15 yrs)	€ 1,00
electricity	€ 4,50 - € 6,50

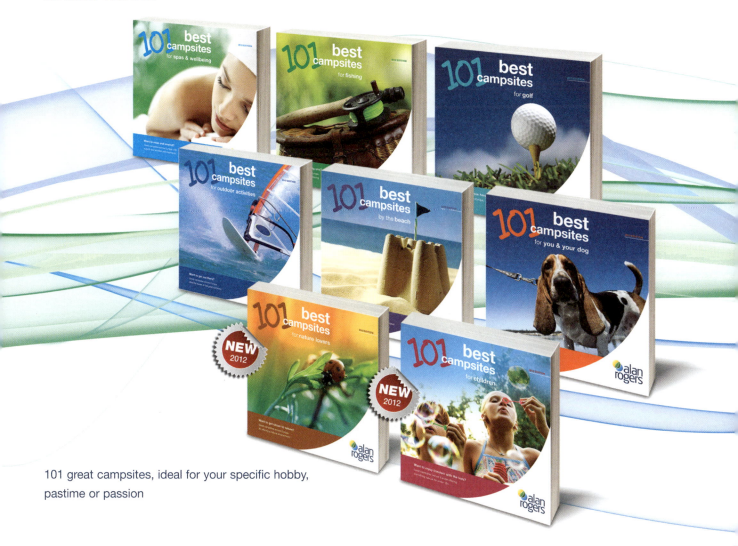

index

index

index